Crayons and Computers

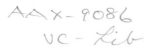

Crayons and Computers

Computer Art Activities for Kids Ages 4 to 8

Carol Sabbeth

CHICAGO
REVIEW
PRESS

Library of Congress Cataloging-in-Publication Data

Sabbeth, Carol, 1957–

    Crayons and computers: a computer art activity book for kids ages 4–8

/ Carol Sabbeth.

        p.   cm.

    Includes bibliographical references.

    ISBN 1-55652-289-4

    1. Art—Study and teaching (Elementary)—Data processing.

2. Color in art. 3. Computer art.   I. Title.

N350.S22 1998

372.5'0285—dc21   97-36764

                                                                                CIP

The author and the publisher of this book disclaim all liability incurred in connection with the use of the information contained in this book.

Cover and interior design by Herman Adler Design Group.

Interior illustrations by Carol Sabbeth and Carol Stutz.

First edition

Published by Chicago Review Press, Incorporated

814 North Franklin Street

Chicago, Illinois 60610

ISBN 1-55652-289-4

Printed in Hong Kong.

By Lammar Offset Printing Ltd.

5 4 3 2 1

To all my colorful friends

Acknowledgments

Many thanks to Chris Fiala Erlich, David Carroll, Priscilla Burton-Roberts, and the kindergarten class at Cornucopia School. I'm also grateful to the many artists who make this book so colorful. Professional artists Nancy Smith Klos and Ron Burns shared their time, knowledge, and artwork. I'm also thankful to the volunteers of the Art Literacy Program and the young artists at Cedaroak and Greenway schools. Special thanks to my husband, Alex, and my editors, Cynthia Sherry and Lisa Rosenthal-Hogarth.

Table of Contents

An Introduction for Parents and Teachers

Today children are growing up with a tool that was a science-fiction fantasy not long ago—the personal computer. While most adults are still trying to master their mouse, kids are whizzing through menus and using keyboard shortcuts as if they were at NASA control. Computers come naturally to kids. So does creativity.

This book combines two things kids love to do: make art projects and use a computer. In this book, children will learn about color as they use their imaginations to express their ideas. They'll experience using a computer as a valuable tool in their creative toolbox. When a computer is added to crayons, glue, and scissors, you get wonderful mixed-media art. Kids will learn that a cyber masterpiece doesn't have to disappear when they hit the "off" switch. Their computer art can be printed out, colored, cut, folded, and glued into many interesting projects.

What You'll Need

The equipment required can be as basic as an old PC or Macintosh that has a color monitor. You'll also need some type of painting or drawing software and any type of printer. Some of the popular paint programs for both Macintosh and Windows are Kid Pix Studio and ClarisWorks. If you have Windows, you already have what you need—an accessory called Paint or Paintbrush. A comparison of these programs is offered here.

Even though this is a book about color, a color printer is only an added bonus. Most projects can be printed in black and white and then colored with traditional tools. Crayons are always listed as the coloring tool, but markers, colored pencils, and paints work great, too. Another way to add color is by printing on colored paper. If you have a CD-ROM and modem with E-mail and Internet access, you can use them, too. In chapter 4, "Colorful Discoveries," you'll find activities that utilize these additions. If time allows, familiarize yourself with the drawing program you've selected before working on the computer with your child or with students.

Computers in the Classroom

These projects work in a classroom setting, too. In a time when funding for art is at an all-time low, it's good to find shelter under the technology umbrella. These projects promote computer training and literacy along with creative thought. Many ideas in this book can be combined with other types of curriculum. (See sidebar for suggestions.) If your classroom is wired to the Internet, make visiting a Web museum, zoo, or aquarium part of a project (see chapter 4 for some Web sites). Your school library probably has art museum CD-ROMs, too. Students can use a CD-ROM to learn about an artist before trying the artist's style. Combine CD-ROMs about zoos and animals with projects in chapter 3, "Mother Nature's Paintbrush."

Let your class put on a cyber art show. Their computer art can be put into an on-screen slide show if you are using Kid Pix Studio or ClarisWorks software.

Comparison of Basic Software Tools and Options

ClarisWorks: The Paint Option

- Freehand pencil
- Eraser
- Pattern fills
- Text
- Slide show
- Rulers
- Transformations such as Rotate, Resize, Flip
- Bitmap Program (See later for Bitmap explanation.)

Pros:

This program has options to do many types of transformations, such as rotate and resize.

ClarisWorks has an option that allows each page of a document to be placed into a slide show. That is, each painting can be viewed on-screen without seeing the program menu or tools. Each page of the document will appear as you click the mouse, or slides can be set to run automatically.

Many Macintosh computers come loaded with ClarisWorks.

Cons

Transformations often require a substantial amount of computer memory.

Text becomes part of the painting; to change it requires erasing.

In the slide show option, every painting must be made in a single document. To begin a new picture, a page is added to the existing document. This creates one very large document (and could slow up an older computer).

Although this program has some good options, it is not easily understood by younger children.

ClarisWorks/Paint uses more computer memory than ClarisWorks/Draw.

ClarisWorks: The Draw Option

- Pattern fills
- Text
- Slide show
- Rulers
- Unpredictable Freehand Pencil
- Transformations such as Rotate, Resize, Flip
- Layering (move to front, move to back)
- Object-Oriented program

Pros

This program has options to do many types of transformations, such as rotate and resize.

Selected objects can be grouped together for easy manipulation.

Text works great. It can be easily altered at any time.

Drawn objects can be easily selected by clicking on them, using the pointer tool.

ClarisWorks has the option of putting each page of a document into a basic slide show. That is, each painting can be viewed on-screen without seeing the program menu or tools. Each page of the file that has a painting will appear as you click the mouse, or slides can be set to run automatically.

Many Macintosh computers come loaded with ClarisWorks.

Cons

Fine details cannot be drawn with the freehand pencil because the drawn line shifts once you release the mouse button.

There is no eraser tool. The entire drawn shape must be deleted to make an alteration.

In the slide show option, every painting must be made in a single document. To begin a new picture, a page is added to the existing document. This makes one very large document (and could slow up an older computer).

Kid Pix Studio

- Freehand pencil
- Eraser
- Pattern fills
- Limited text options
- Slide show
- Stamps
- Bitmap program

Pros

Kid Pix was designed for young children and is easy for them to use. The stamp tool provides predrawn images which can be added to a drawing.

Paintings can be made in separate documents, then compiled in an easy-to-use slide show. Sounds can be added to the show, too. Along with a painting program, the Studio version of Kid Pix has other multimedia options to explore.

Cons

There is a lot of animation in this program to capture a child's attention. It may distract from the task of drawing.

Some kids will use only predrawn stamps in their creation. They do not draw original art. This program does not have the option to flip, rotate, or resize an object.

Windows Paint or Paintbrush

- Freehand pencil
- Eraser
- Text
- Rulers (on Paint version)
- Bitmap program
- Transformations such as Rotate, Resize, Flip

Pros

If you have Windows on your P.C., this program is already on your computer (in the Accessories menu).

Options such as rotate and flip are available.

Cons

There are no pattern fills available in this program.

There is no option for viewing artwork on-screen in a slide show.

Paintbrush does not have a measuring tool. Paint does.

Software Comparison Chart

	ClarisWorks/Paint	ClarisWorks/Draw	Kid Pix Studio	Windows Paint/Paintbrush
Pattern Fills	●	●	●	
Rotate, Flip, etc.	●	●		●
Text	●	●	Limited	●
Pencil	●	Limited	●	●
Eraser	●		●	●
Rulers	●	●		◗ (in Paint only)
Move to...(layers)		●		
Stamps			●	
Slide Show	Limited	Limited	●	
Bitmapped	●		●	●
Object-Oriented		●		
Ease of use	4	3	1	2

This chart shows how some of the tools and options compare between software programs. Listed here are some of the more important functions—those that would be helpful in making projects in this book. Other tools and options are also available in all of the programs. (1 = easiest to use; 4 = most difficult)

A Quick Lesson about Software

Images can be made on a computer in two ways; they are often referred to as "painting" programs and "drawing" programs. There is a difference in the way each works. Understanding the difference will help you when using the program.

A painting program uses a system called *bitmapping* to display images on the screen. As an artist working in a bitmap program, you will be able to draw squiggles and shapes on the screen and then erase any part of them with an eraser tool. Images can also be moved around. Moving or erasing a shape you painted on top of something else will leave an empty space.

Text works the same way. It is not like word processing. In a paint program, if you make a typing error, you must erase it and start over (you cannot insert a cursor to make corrections).

Drawing programs, on the other hand, are "object-oriented." When working in an object-oriented program, you will not be able to erase small parts of a squiggle or shape. There is no eraser tool. You'll have to select and delete the entire squiggle. You select the squiggle by clicking on it with a pointer tool. You know the image is selected by the little boxes, called "grabber handles" that appear. In many low-cost drawing programs, the squiggle you draw will distort slightly. This could be a problem if you are drawing fine details.

Text is easier to work with in a drawing program because it can be altered at any time by using a cursor tool. Think of an object-oriented picture as you would a picture made of cut paper shapes. They can overlap each other and can be moved around easily, too.

One way to tell which category your program falls into is by its name. Does it have the words "Paint" or "Draw" in its title? Many of the software products developed for children's art, such as Kid Pix, are bitmapped. (Note: Most of the projects in this book would work best with software that uses bitmapping.)

A Guide to Combining Computers, Art, and Other Curriculum

Several projects in this book can be combined with other subjects you are teaching. Here are a few suggestions.

Creative Writing
- Colorful Days Diary, page 46
- Autumn Leaves, page 35

Learning Basic Shapes
- Crazy Shapes, page 80

Science and Nature
- Design a Habitat, page 110
- Find the Fish, page 106
- Magical Aquarium, page 108
- Bathtub Buddy, page 100
- Monarch Butterfly Magnet, page 99
- Sea Garden, page 124

Marketing and Design
- My Own Cookie Company, page 24

Music
- Marimba Mouse, page 9
- Cool, Calm Creations, page 14
- Rhythm Shaker, page 10
- Imagination Station, page 86

Internet Research
- Mona Lisa and Me, page 121
- Crayons and Computers in Cyberspace, page 129

E-mail
- Send an E-mail Masterpiece, page 126

CD-ROM Research
- Zoo Safari Game, page 134

Before You Begin

This book is full of great projects you can make. There's one thing all the projects have in common—your computer. You can use either a Macintosh computer or a PC that has Windows.

All the drawings are done using a mouse and a computer. When the directions for a project tell you to "Draw a . . ." it means to draw it on your computer. After you've drawn a picture, you'll print it. You can use either a color or black-and-white printer. Most of the time you'll print onto white paper. When a special color of paper is needed, this will be listed under "materials." If you don't have a color printer, you can add color with all sorts of things. The materials specify crayons, but you can use paints, colored pencils, markers, anything! It's fun to try out different materials. Even if you print in color, you can add your own touch with extra colors. Experiment! Most of all, have fun.

Happy coloring!

1. Colorful Fun

The world is a very colorful place. Bright, cheery colors are everywhere. It's nice to know there are so many colors to choose from when we make a picture. Coloring a picture is a big part of being an artist. That's because color is one of the first things someone notices about a picture. An artist can make her pictures scream loudly or whisper softly by the colors she uses. Learning more about colors and how to use them in your drawings will make doing art more fun.

Red, Yellow, Blue... What You Can Do

How many colors do you think there are?
A big box of crayons holds almost a hundred colors.
You can make all sorts of colors at
your computer, too.

Mother Nature's Color Wheel

Next time you see a rainbow, take a closer look. You'll notice that the colors in the rainbow match the colors in the color wheel. They're even in the same order. The top color will be red, then you'll see orange, yellow, green, blue, and purple.

Believe it or not, there are really only three simple colors. All the other colors are made from mixing these three colors together. Different recipes will make different colors. These three simple colors are red, yellow, and blue. They are called the *primary colors*. Primary means first, or beginning.

To get three more colors, just mix two primary colors together. If you mix red and yellow together, you'll get orange. If you mix yellow and blue together, you'll get green. And blue and red will make purple. Now you have three more colors. These new colors—orange, green, and purple—came second. These are called the *secondary colors*.

These six colors can be painted in a circle or wheel. This is called a *color wheel*. Each color has a certain place on the wheel depending on its recipe. Green sits between blue and yellow on the wheel because it is made up of these two colors. Artists think about the color wheel a lot. Where each color sits on the wheel is important.

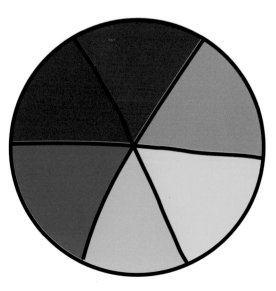

Flying Colors

Here's a project where you can make a kite of rainbow colors. It's also a color wheel that you can use when you're painting.

Materials

- **Ruler**
- **Computer printer paper**
- **6 crayons: red, orange, yellow, green, blue, and purple**
- **Scissors**
- **Ribbon**
- **Stapler**

1. In the middle of the screen, draw a straight 6-inch line across the page, from left to right.

2. Draw 2 more lines; start each line at one end of the 6-inch line and drag, on an angle, to the top of the page. Repeat this, but do it so the lines meet at the bottom of the page. You should end up with 2 triangles, making a diamond shape.

3. Draw a big *X* inside the diamond to cut each triangle into 3 wedges. Your diamond is now divided into 6 wedges. Print 1 copy.

4. Color each wedge in this order: red, orange, yellow, green, blue, and purple. It doesn't matter which wedge you color first so long as you color them in this order.

5. Cut out the diamond shape.

6. Cut 3 pieces of ribbon, each 10 inches long. Staple these pieces of ribbon to one point of the diamond to make a tail for your kite.

If you like, hang your kite near your computer so you can use it as your color wheel for reference.

Stained Glass Window

Let's use the computer monitor like a window. It lights up the "stained glass" as you create a piece of art. Notice how many extra colors you see when you overlap the colored tissues. If you put a yellow tissue on top of a red tissue, the overlapped area will look orange. This is just like mixing paints to get new colors.

Materials

- **3 pieces of tissue paper of different colors**
- **Ruler**
- **Scissors**
- **Clear plastic tape**
- **Computer printer paper**
- **Glue stick**
- **Crayons**

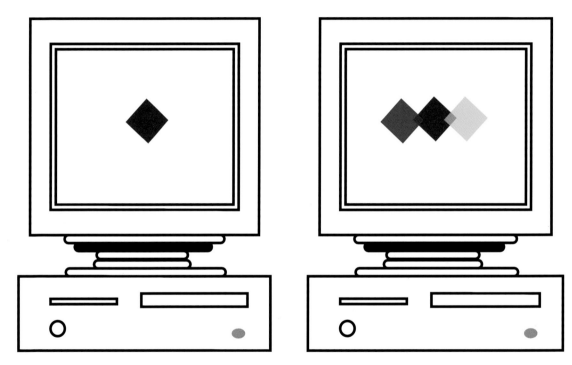

1. Cut a 2-inch square from each piece of tissue paper.

2. Turn your computer monitor on and open a new file in your paint program. Place a tissue paper square, with corners pointing up and down, in the center of the screen. It should cling on its own, but if it doesn't, secure it with a small piece of tape. Place a second tissue paper square to the left of the first, overlapping it a little. Add the third square to the right, overlapping this one, too.

3. Use your drawing tools to add stems and leaves to the tissue squares so that they look like flowers.

4. Add other details to your drawing, such as a sky or trees. Then print it out.

5. Remove the tissue paper from your monitor. Apply glue to one side of a tissue square and press it onto the printed page on top of one of the printed stems. Do this for the other 2 pieces of tissue paper and stems.

6. Use crayons to color in the other images you drew on this page.

7. Hang your stained glass picture in a window to see the tissue colors light up.

Rainbow Quilt

Make a colorful quilt using the six basic colors in your computer's paint palette.

1. Draw a large square. An easy way to make a square is to hold down the shift key while you drag on an angle with the rectangle tool.

2. Draw a big *X* inside the square, from corner to corner.

3. Draw a line across the center of the square. The square is now divided into 6 wedges.

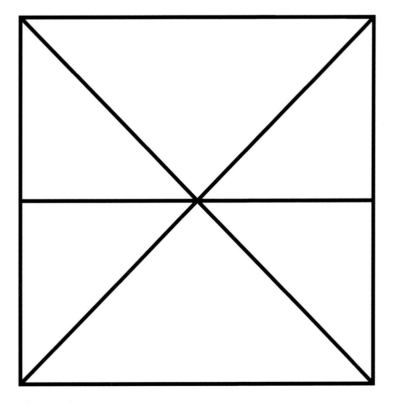

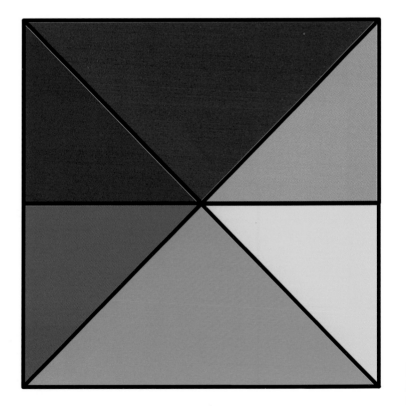

4. Use the paint bucket tool to color each wedge in this order: red, orange, yellow, green, blue, and purple. It doesn't matter which wedge you start in.

5. Draw a small picture in each wedge of anything that reminds you of that color. For example, draw a heart in the red square and orange trees in the orange square.

6. Enjoy your quilt on-screen, or print it out. If you print your quilt in black ink, use your crayons to make a colorful border around the square using the color of each wedge along the side of that wedge.

What Is a Paint Palette?

Artists like to have all their colors ready to use and waiting when they paint. So, they squeeze a small amount of each color they plan to use onto a flat tray. This tray is called a *palette*. Many palettes have a thumbhole in them. The palette is held in one hand while the artist paints using the other hand. Painters often put the colors in a certain order on their palette. Keeping them in order makes the colors easier to find.

The word palette is also used in computer painting lingo. It's the area where all the color choices are found. Look at the paint palette on your computer. The colors are in a special order. Sometimes the six primary and secondary colors are together, or maybe colors that are similar, such as peach and orange, are grouped together. How are the colors on your computer palette arranged?

Colors Have a Temperature

Let's take a closer look at the color wheel. Red, orange, and yellow sit next to each other. These three colors are called *warm* colors. Think of the color of the bright yellow-orange sun and of a red-hot fire. This is how you can remember the colors that are warm. Warm colors are exciting! If you paint with warm colors, your picture will make people want to jump up and dance.

Now look at the other half of the color wheel. You'll see that green, blue, and purple sit next to each other. These colors are called *cool* colors. Think of a green hillside, a blue lake, and a purple mountain. Cool colors are peaceful. If you paint a picture using cool colors, it will make people feel calm and relaxed.

Marimba Mouse

Here's a fun way to practice using the warm colors in your paint palette. Dance to a lively beat while you mambo with your mouse.

* **Radio playing lively music**

1. Move the chair away from your computer desk.

2. Stand in front of your computer and move to the lively music playing on the radio.

3. Create a picture using only the reds, oranges, and yellows in your paint palette. This picture doesn't need to be realistic. Maybe you just want to make bright, colorful splashes. See what you can create before the end of a song.

Rhythm Shaker

Become a part of the lively music you hear. First make, then shake, this rhythm instrument. You can have a rhythm jam while a friend takes his turn mamboing with the mouse.

Materials

- **Ruler**
- **Computer printer paper**
- **Crayons in reds, oranges, and yellows**
- **Scissors**
- **Glue stick**
- **1 soft drink can, empty**
- **Uncooked popcorn**
- **Masking tape**

1. Draw a 5-inch-tall rectangle across the width of your page.

2. Draw a tropical design inside the rectangle using lines only; do not add colors. You can draw a sun, palm trees, the ocean, or anything else that looks hot and tropical. Print 1 copy.

3. Color your design with reds, oranges, and yellows. Cut out the rectangle and glue it around an empty soft drink can.

4. Pour a handful of popcorn into the can. Tape the opening shut.

Shake your rhythm shaker while imagining you're on a beach by the ocean. Can you smell the salty air? Can you feel a warm ocean breeze? Do you feel the warmth of the sun?

Keeping in Line

It's fun to experiment with all the colors on your computer. It's also fun to combine computer drawing with other types of paints or materials. Artists call this *mixed media*. It's a great way to add color if you don't have a color printer. Even if you do have a color printer, try using crayons, markers, cut paper, magazine pictures, or just about anything to add color to your printed piece. One way to use mixed media is to draw the outlines of pictures on your computer. The art will look like a page from a coloring book. Print out the picture and then color it. You can print extra copies of your line art and give them to friends or a little brother or sister to color.

Curly Birds

Make a chirpy pal who can perch on top of your monitor. His warm colors will brighten your day.

Materials

- **Computer printer paper**
- **Crayons in reds, oranges, and yellows**
- **Scissors**
- **Glue stick**

1. Draw the pattern pieces for the bird's head, body, feet, and crest on the computer. Draw with outlines only; don't add color.

2. Add designs and patterns to decorate the bird. Print 1 copy.

3. Color the pieces with warm colors. Turn the body piece over and color its reverse side, too.

4. Cut the pieces out. Cut slits in the tail end of the body and in the crest, to make feathers.

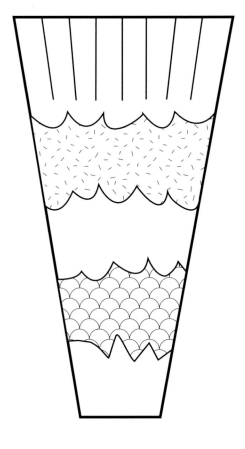

5. One at a time, roll the head, crest, and body around a crayon to make them curl.

6. Use a glue stick to glue the narrow end of the body to the tip of the middle tail feather as shown.

7. Glue the crest on the head, the head to the body, and then the feet to the underside of the body.

Cool, Calm Creations

The cool colors make you feel calm and relaxed. Practice using greens, blues, and purples while you listen to mellow music.

Materials

•   **Radio playing slow, calm music**

1. Sit in front of your computer with your eyes closed and listen to the music playing on the radio. Take big, slow breaths and relax for a minute or more.

2. Open your eyes and begin to paint. Use only the greens, blues, and purples in your paint palette to paint a picture. The picture can be a realistic scene of a grassy hill next to a big cool lake, or the picture can be abstract; that is, make designs using soft round shapes.

Cool-Colored Fan

This cool-colored fan will cool you off
on a hot summer day.

Materials

- **Light blue or green computer printer paper**
- **Crayons in greens, blues, and purples**
- **Scissors**

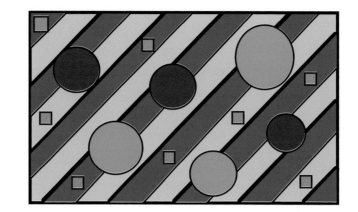

1. Draw a rectangle that covers your drawing area.

2. Using lines, circles, and squares, draw a design inside the rectangle.

3. Put 1 sheet of colored paper into the printer and print 1 copy.

4. Color your design with greens, blues, and purples.

5. Cut out the colored rectangle.

6. Fold the rectangle accordion-style, starting the fold at a shorter edge. Fold the entire rectangle. Pinch the bottom of the folded piece and fan the top out.

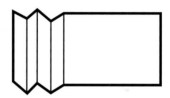

Now you're ready to cool off! Wave your fan in front of your face and enjoy the cool breeze.

Night and Day Zigzag

Bright, cheery, warm colors are often used to show sunny days. If you use darker shades of cool colors, you can paint a night scene. Make two versions of the same scene, one during the day-time and one at night. Put them together in a zigzag sculpture.

Materials

- **Computer printer paper**
- **Color printer or crayons**
- **Scissors**
- **Ruler**
- **Pen or pencil**
- **1 piece of thin cardboard (from a man's dress shirt)**
- **Glue stick**

1. Draw a large rectangle on your screen. Inside the rectangle, draw a picture of your house. Make the drawing in outline only; don't add color. Save this picture as "Outline." (If you have a black-and-white printer, print 2 copies now. Color 1 picture with cool colors and 1 picture with warm colors only. Next, go to step 4.)

2. On-screen, use greens, blues, and purples to color your picture as if it is nighttime. Save this file as "Night." Print 1 color copy.

3. Open the file named "Outline" and color this picture as if it is daytime. Use reds, oranges, and yellows. Save this file as "Day." Print 1 color copy.

4. Cut out both pictures along the large rectangle.

5. Use a ruler and pen or pencil to measure the height and width of your picture. Cut out a piece of cardboard that is the same height as one of your pictures, but twice its width. (For example, if each picture is 6 inches wide by 4 inches high, cut a piece of cardboard that is 12 inches by 4 inches.)

6. Fold the width of each picture into accordion-style pleats, each about 1 inch wide. Cut the pictures into strips, along the folds. Keep the strips in their correct order.

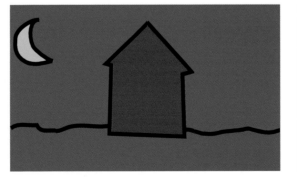

7. Glue the first strip from one picture to the end of the piece of cardboard. Glue the first strip from the other picture next. Keep gluing strips until both pictures are on the long piece of cardboard.

8. Fold the cardboard into an accordion along each strip. Stand the art on its bottom edge to see your house at day. Look from the other way to see it at night.

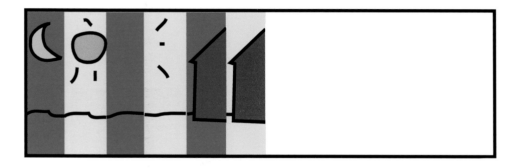

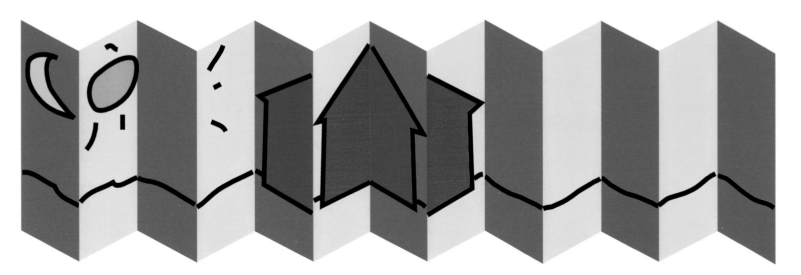

Mix It Up with Warm and Cool Color Combinations

Paintings that really stand out have both warm and cool colors in them. A painting colored red and blue is much more vivid than one painted red and yellow. This is because there is more of a difference between red and blue. This difference is called *contrast*. Warm colors have more contrast when they are next to cool colors.

Here's a little test to take. Look at the three green squares on this page. Each square has another color set into it. Which combination stands out the most? Most people would say the orange and green combination stands out the most. The blue and purple squares are less noticeable when next to green. These are cool-color combinations that have less contrast. The orange and green combination has more contrast because orange is a warm color and green is a cool color.

Panama Pizzazz

These brightly colored designs are made by the Cuna women who live in Panama and Columbia. This piece is called a *mola*. Mola appliqué is a technique for making decorative clothing by tacking together two or more layers of fabric in different colors. These colorful panels are sewn to the fronts and backs of blouses.

The project on the following pages will show you how warm and cool colors affect one another. As you'll see, the blue and purple shapes will appear much brighter against a yellow background.

Panama Pizzazz (continued)

After viewing the mola on the previous page, follow the steps to make your own. Be sure to use warm and cool colors.

Materials

- **Blue, purple, and yellow computer printer paper**
- **Scissors**
- **Glue stick**

1. Draw a circle the size of a quarter in the center of the screen.

2. Draw a petal shape $\frac{1}{2}$ inch outside this circle.

3. Draw another petal shape $\frac{1}{2}$ inch outside this first one. Finally, draw a third petal shape $\frac{1}{2}$ inch outside the last one drawn.

4. Place 1 sheet each of blue, purple, and yellow paper into the printer tray. Print 3 copies of the pattern on your screen.

5. Look at the diagram on this page to see how each shape is numbered. From the blue piece of paper, cut out shapes 1 and 5. You will not use these pieces.

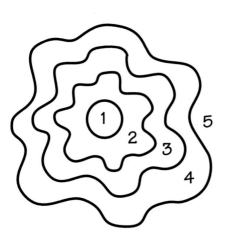

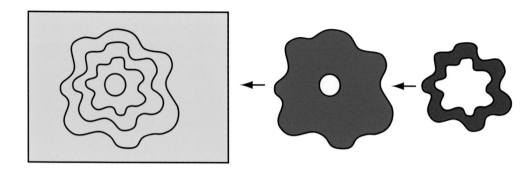

6. From the purple piece of paper, cut shapes 1, 2, 4, and 5. Put these shapes to one side; you will not use them.

7. Apply glue to the back of the blue shape; place it on top of the same shape on the yellow paper.

8. Apply glue to the back of the purple shape; press this piece on top and in the middle of the blue shape.

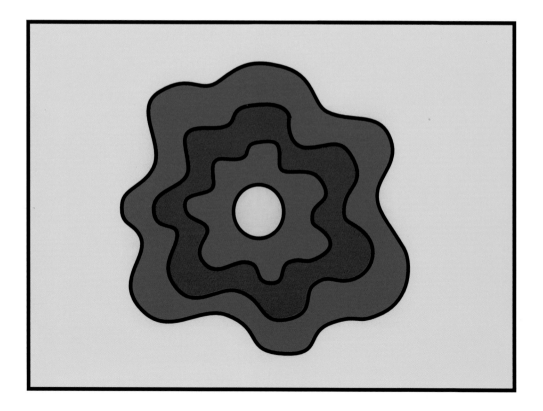

Colorful ABCs

Practice typing your ABCs while making a colorful sign for your bedroom. This activity will also give you the chance to see how warm and cool colors look on the computer screen.

Materials

- **White computer printer paper**
- **Scissors**
- **Blue, purple, and yellow computer printer paper**
- **Glue stick**

1. Draw a bright blue rectangle across your screen. Draw a smaller purple rectangle inside the blue shape. Notice how blue and purple look together on the screen. Because they are both cool colors, they are not a very vivid combination.

2. Select Text from your tool palette and, from the Text menu, set the type to be bold (and large, an option on some programs). On some programs, under the Text menu, you can change the *font*—the look of the alphabet characters—and adjust the size of the letters here. Next, click on the color yellow from your color palette.

3. Click the typing cursor inside the purple rectangle and begin typing the letters of the alphabet. Hit the Enter key.

4. Type your name and a message, too. Notice how bright the yellow letters look when they are against the purple background. That's because purple is a cool color and yellow is a warm color.

ABCDEFGHIJKLMNOPQRSTUVWXYZ
JASON'S ROOM

5. On white paper, print out the art in color, or print it using black ink. Cut out the large rectangle.

6. Add a colorful border made from blue, purple, and yellow paper. Cut a rectangle that is larger than your artwork from 1 color. Glue the art to this background. Cut small shapes out of the remaining 2 colors and glue them onto the border surrounding your artwork.

ABCDEFGHIJKLMNOPQRSTUVWXYZ
JASON'S ROOM

Crazy Keyboard

You might wonder why the letters are so mixed up on your computer's keyboard. To understand, you have to picture the big clunky typewriter that was used a long time ago. If you looked inside this old typewriter, you would see many tiny hammers. One letter of the alphabet was at the head of each hammer. The very first keyboards were designed with the letters of the alphabet in the correct order. If a person typed too fast, the hammers would hit each other and stick together. The design had to be changed to keep the keys from jamming. The crazy keyboard we use today was originally designed to slow us down. Today's keyboard is called "QWERTY." Can you guess why?

My Own Cookie Company

Make a cookie jar with your own designer label. Decorate the label using both warm and cool colors to make it bright and cheery.

Materials

- Computer printer paper
- Scissors
- Crayons
- Large, empty jar with lid (like a mayonnaise container or pickle jar)
- Glue stick
- Hole puncher or pencil
- Ribbon

1. Draw a large square on the computer screen. Draw another square inside the first one to make a nice-sized border.

2. Inside the square, type the name of your cookie company in large letters. Add a picture or design to your label. Draw this picture in outline only; do not color it.

3. Print 1 copy of your design. Cut it out.

4. Color your label with crayons using both warm and cool colors.

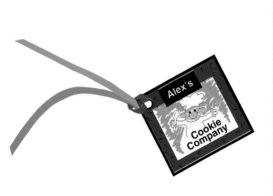

5. Prepare the jar by removing any labels. This can be done by soaking it in hot water. Wash, rinse, and dry the jar.

6. Apply glue to the back of the label you made on the computer, and press the label onto the jar.

7. Fill your cookie jar with your favorite treats.

Here's another idea: Set your printer to print this same image in a smaller size. (Kid Pix Studio calls this "Itsy Bitsy" size. In Paint or Paintbrush, change the scaling on the Print menu to 50 percent.) This will make a mini label that can be used as a gift tag. Print it out, and then color it. Use a hole puncher or a pencil to make a hole in one corner. Poke a ribbon through this hole and tie it around a big cookie covered in plastic wrap. Everyone will love this delicious surprise!

Supermarket Snoop

Go to the cereal aisle next time you go to the grocery store. This can be the brightest place in the store. What kinds of colors do you see on the cereal boxes? The boxes are often yellow or orange. Even the words on the box are brightly colored. If a new type of cereal came in a box that was drab green or muddy gray, would you buy it? Probably not.

People who design packages for products spend a lot of time studying colors and deciding which ones to use. Color is very important when it comes to selling a product. Sometimes manufacturers test new packaging ideas out on small groups of people before they make a final decision.

While you're at the market, go to the fruit and vegetable section. The grocer *could* place the lemons, bananas, and yellow apples next to each other. Why do you think he doesn't? How does mixing the colors affect how the produce looks?

Complementary Colors

Colors that sit across from each other on the color wheel make the most exciting combinations of all. When they are used together, they really grab your attention. Colors that are opposite each other on the color wheel are called *complementary colors*. The complementary colors on the color wheel are red and green, yellow and purple, and orange and blue. When used together, these colors are so vivid that sometimes they seem to vibrate.

Chad Jones, age 10

Woven Heart

Weave a beautiful heart of complementary colors. Hang it as a decoration or fill it with candy. This heart-shaped ornament is a little basket. The weaving is a bit tricky at first, but it can be done with an adult's help. Once you get the hang of it, make more hearts using different color combinations.

Materials

- Computer printer paper
- 2 crayons of complementary colors
- Scissors

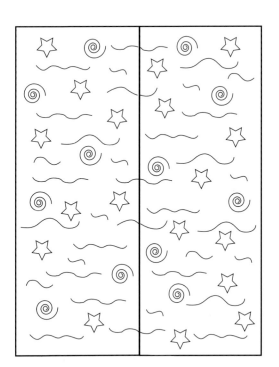  

1. Draw a rectangle that is twice as long as it is wide. Draw a line down the center of the rectangle, dividing it in equal halves.

2. Decorate the rectangle with designs. Print 1 copy.

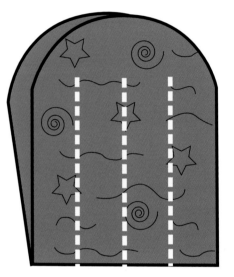

3. Color one half of the rectangle using a red, blue, or yellow crayon. Color the other half with its complementary color. Cut the rectangle in half, down the middle line.

4. Fold each length in half and cut, from the folded end, into 3 equal strips, to within 1 inch of the edge (close but not quite all the way through the paper).

5. Cut a curve on the open ends of each folded rectangle.

6. Follow the diagram to weave the two pieces together.

Colorful Seasons

Look for complementary colors in nature.
You can find them in the summer, winter, spring,
and fall. These projects use complementary
colors from each season.

Spring Bouquet

Pick a bouquet of yellow and purple flowers. Maybe you have a flower garden with yellow tulips and purple lilacs. If not, make a bouquet of paper pansies. You'll need a special vase for your bouquet. Surprise your mom with this colorful gift on Mother's Day, or give it to someone who loves flowers, just because.

Materials

- **Ruler**
- **Computer printer paper**
- **Scissors**
- **Crayons**
- **Glue stick**
- **1 15-ounce tin can, washed with lid removed**
- **Yellow and purple flowers**

1. Use the ruler to measure the height of a tin can. Draw a rectangle large enough to fit around and cover the entire tin can.

2. Decorate the rectangle on-screen with springtime designs, drawn with outlines only. Print 1 copy.

3. Cut out the rectangle and color it using crayons.

4. Apply glue to the back of the artwork and press it around the tin can.

5. Fill the can with water and add freshly picked yellow and purple flowers.

Pansy Bouquet

If you'd like to make paper flowers for your spring bouquet (previous activity), place a scrunched-up plastic bag inside the can to hold these flowers in place.

Materials

- Computer printer paper
- Scissors
- 2 crayons: yellow and purple
- Clear plastic tape
- Garbage bag twist ties

1. Draw a pansy shape. Use the Copy and Paste functions to make duplicate flowers until your page is filled. Print 1 copy.

2. Cut out all the pansy shapes.

3. Color each flower yellow and purple. Turn the flowers over and color the reverse sides, using only 1 color.

4. Tape a twist tie to the back of each flower. Place the flowers in your springtime vase.

A Slice of Summer

A big slice of watermelon is a perfect example of how bright the color red looks when it's next to green. You can use this example of nature's design to make brightly colored name tags for your next summer barbecue.

Materials

- **Ruler**
- **Red and green computer printer paper**
- **Scissors**
- **Glue stick**
- **Toothpicks**
- **Clear plastic tape**

1. Draw a slice of watermelon about 4 inches tall and 5 inches wide. Add a curved line $\frac{1}{2}$ inch from the bottom, to show where the watermelon rind starts.

2. Type a name or message in the wedge and draw some seeds.

3. Put 1 sheet of green and 1 sheet of red paper in your printer and print 2 copies of your picture.

4. Cut out the entire shape from the green piece of paper. Cut the upper wedge (without the rind portion) from the red piece of paper.

5. Glue the red wedge on top of the green shape.

6. Tape a toothpick to the back of the watermelon on the bottom so that part of the toothpick is showing.

If you make one for everybody, you can use this as a place marker at your next barbecue by gently pushing each toothpick through a paper tablecloth. Or you can personalize dessert by sticking 1 marker in each piece of cake, ice cream, or watermelon!

Autumn Leaves

Autumn is a time of colorful leaves and pumpkin patches. Write a story or poem about what you like about autumn, and turn it into a piece of art.

Materials

- **1 piece of blue computer printer paper**
- **Glue stick**
- **Orange leaves**

1. Go outside and stand under a bright orange tree. See how pretty it looks against the blue sky. Pick up a few leaves that have fallen from one of its branches.

2. Think of a story or poem that expresses what you like best about the fall.

3. At your computer, type your short story or poem. The text shouldn't take up more than half the page. Print 1 copy on blue paper.

4. Apply glue to 1 side of an orange leaf. Decorate your story by pressing the glued leaf onto the printed page next to your story or poem. Add more leaves if you'd like.

I rake my leaves
into a bunch.
Then jump on it
to hear them
crunch.

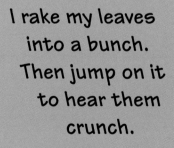

I rake my leaves
into a bunch.
Then jump on it
to hear them
crunch.

Winter Wreath of Hearts and Hugs

Winter is the time to see green holly bushes full of red berries. Here's a colorful wreath made of green leaves and red hearts. Each heart's message promises a little gift from you. Make a heart wreath for someone special and give it to her on Valentine's Day. Your valentine can pluck a heart whenever she's ready to receive a gift.

Materials

- **Red and green computer printer paper**
- **Scissors**
- **Glue stick**
- **Clear plastic tape**
- **Ribbon**

1. Use the pencil tool to draw 4 large hearts.

2. Think of 4 little gifts you'd like to give your valentine. A gift could be a great big hug or a little chore such as setting the table. Type the name of 1 gift in each of the hearts. Add decorations, too.

3. Print 1 copy on red paper. Cut out each heart.

4. Open a new file. Draw a large circle. Draw a second circle inside the first, leaving about 1 inch between the circles. This is the base of your wreath.

5. Draw about 10 leaves in the open drawing area outside the circles.

6. Print 1 copy on green paper. Cut out each piece. Throw away the inner circle; you will use the large open circle.

7. Apply glue to the back of each leaf and stick it onto the large circle.

8. Roll a piece of tape into a ring. Put 1 ring of tape on the back of each heart. Stick each heart onto the wreath.

9. Tape a piece of looped ribbon onto the back of the wreath at the top. This is how you can hang your wreath.

Your valentine can remove one heart at a time, whenever she is ready for her gift.

Blooming Flowers

Strange things can happen when you use complementary colors. Here is a little experiment to try out.

Materials

- **Color printer, if available**
- **Computer printer paper**

1. Draw a big yellow daisy with a black center on one side of the screen. Add a green stem and leaves. (One side of the screen should remain blank.)

2. Look at the daisy's black center while counting to 20. Then, look at the empty part of the screen. What do you see? I bet you saw a daisy that is colored differently.

3. If you have a color printer, print your artwork and repeat the experiment.

What did you see? The new daisy might have looked purple while its stem and leaves looked red. This is because purple is the complementary color of yellow, and red is the complement of green. When we look at a color too long our eyes get tired and switch colors.

Give Your Eyes a Break

Look away from your computer screen every now and then while you're working. This will give your eyes a rest. Your eyes become tired when you look at anything too intensely for a long period of time. This even happens when you read a book.

Crayons of Every Color

The color wheel can be made of many more colors than the six on our circle. Colors are mixed together in different recipes to get more and more choices. It's hard to believe that it all started with red, yellow, and blue. If you look in a box of crayons you'll see colors with names like Blue Green, Turquoise, and Aqua. All three of these colors are a kind of blue. The colors you can paint with on your computer don't have names, but they are just as varied. Look at your computer paint palette and see how many types of blue you can find.

There's a spot on the color wheel for all of these blues. There are also many types of reds, purples, greens, and browns. No matter how large your color wheel is, each color has a complementary color across from it on the circle.

The Crayola Story

The first box of Crayola crayons appeared in 1903. It had only eight colors in it: red, yellow, blue, orange, green, purple, black, and brown. Over the years, the color choices grew until the big box of 96 colors was created. Fun names like Asparagus and Tickle Me Pink were born. Some names were changed, too. Prussian Blue was changed to Midnight Blue when teachers told the makers of Crayola Crayons that students were no longer familiar with the history of Prussia. They also changed the name of the color called Flesh to Peach after they realized that people come in many different colors.

Tickled Pink— Tints and Shades

Colors like pink and lilac are made when you add white to a color. Pink is made when white is added to red. When you add white to purple, you get lilac. Pink and lilac are called *tints*. Sometimes tints are called pastel colors. Darker colors, such as dark red and dark purple, can be made by adding black. When you add black to a color, the new color is called a *shade*. Here's a little trick to remember the difference between a tint and a shade:

A tint has a hint, but a shade does not fade.

Bubble Words

The colors of a soap bubble are so light, they look like tints. In this project you'll make a bubbly greeting with tints of the primary and secondary colors. Try it out with the tinted colors in your computer paint palette. Explore the tints your crayon box holds, too. Once you get the hang of writing in bubbles, make a piece of bubble art of your name.

Materials

- **Computer printer paper**
- **Crayons**

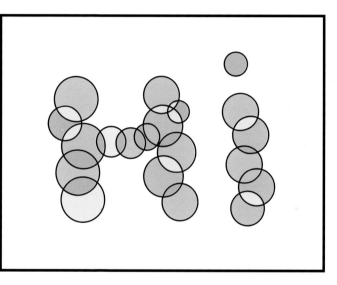

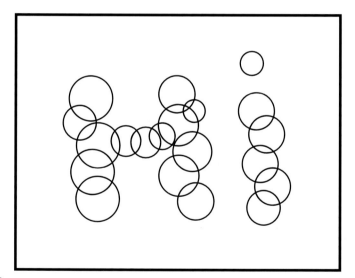

1. Use the oval tool to make an unfilled circle about the size of a nickel. (Hold down the shift key while dragging the oval tool to make a circle.) Make several circles, overlapping them a bit, until they form the letter "H." Make the letter "i" also.

2. Print 1 copy of the art while the circles are still uncolored. Set this copy to the side while you finish your computer art.

3. Explore your computer paint palette to find colors that are tints. Use the paint bucket or paint roller icon to fill in the circles with these light colors. Print 1 copy. If you have a color printer, the tints will be in various colors. If you have a black-and-white printer, the tints will all appear light and dark gray. This is called *grayscale*.

4. Pull out all the tints you can find in your crayon box. You'll find colors such as pink, lavender, light blue, and pale green. Use these crayons to color the bubbles on the first page you printed.

Crayon Batik Goody Box

Make a little box to keep your treasures in. You'll see how adding black ink over your artwork gives it a darker, shaded look. This method of adding color over waxed areas is called *batik* (buh-TEEK). It comes to us from Indonesia. Batik artists paint wax on fabric, then dip the material in colorful dyes. Beautiful patterns emerge when the wax is melted away.

Materials

- **Computer printer paper**
- **Crayons (required)**
- **Newspaper**
- **Black ink**
- **Paintbrush**
- **Facial tissue**
- **Small shoe box with lid**
- **Poster paint**
- **Scissors**
- **Glue stick**

Jordan Melland, age 10

1. Draw a simple picture using thick black lines. Do not add color. Print 1 copy.

2. Use crayons to color the areas between the black lines. Be sure to fill in all the white spaces. Crunch the artwork into a ball, then flatten it out.

3. Place newspaper on a tabletop and your artwork on top of the newspaper. Paint over the entire artwork with ink. The ink will not stick well to areas where the wax from the crayon covers the paper. Dab the ink puddles with a tissue to dry the page. You'll notice that the black ink has mixed with some of the colors. You've created a shaded look.

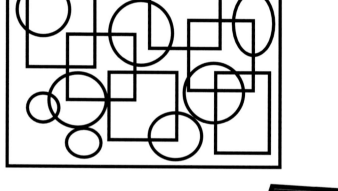

Crayon Batik Goody Box (continued)

4. Prepare the shoe box and lid by painting them with bright colors. Let the pieces dry.

5. Trim the artwork to fit the lid of the shoe box. Apply glue to the back of the art and glue it to the lid.

Painting with Light

To some artists, the contrast of light and dark was the most important part of a picture. These painters thought more about the lightness and darkness of their paintings than about bright colors. When you look at their paintings, you see brightly lit faces against dark backgrounds. It's as if a spotlight is shining on one part of the painting. This way of painting is called *chiaroscuro* (kee-AHR-eh-SKUUR-oh). That's Italian meaning "light and dark." A Dutch artist named Rembrandt became famous for his chiaroscuro style.

School of Sir Anthony Van Dyck
François Duquesnoy
Oil on canvas, 29 in. x $23\frac{1}{4}$ in.
Gift of Mr. Val A. Browning
Utah Museum of Fine Arts

How Colors Make You Feel

We know that warm colors are exciting and cool colors are relaxing. Each color by itself makes us feel a certain way, too. Have you heard the expression "being green with envy" or heard that someone has "the blues"? Some scientists study how colors make us feel. This information is used by interior decorators, florists, and just about everyone who uses color in their work. Artists also think a lot about colors and emotions. They often use a particular color in a picture to tell a story or send a message. Here's what scientists have discovered about how a particular color might make us feel:

red = excitement

yellow = happiness

blue = calmness

green = life

orange = energy

purple = mystery

Colorful Days Diary

How do different colors make you feel? Maybe you feel silly and orange. Does a bright yellow day make you smile? Think about how your feelings can be described by a color and make a little book from your ideas. You'll get to practice typing the days of the week and names of colors. Have fun thinking of a little rhyme to go with your colorful feeling and include it in your book.

Materials

- **Colored computer printer paper**
- **Hole puncher or pencil**
- **Yarn**

Saturday, yeah! I get to play. It's a lively orange day.

1. Draw a picture about Monday. Add words to the page about Monday such as "On Monday I feel pink." Add a little rhyme to the story if you'd like. Print 1 copy on a sheet of paper that is the color you use for this day.

2. Repeat step 1 for each day of the week.

Saturday, yeah! I get to play. It's a lively orange day.

MY COLOR-FILLED DAYS

3. Design a cover for your book. Print 1 copy on your favorite color paper.

4. Stack all the pages in the order of their days of the week.

5. Punch 2 holes along the left side of each page.

6. Thread the holes with a piece of yarn and tie the yarn in a bow or knot.

Telling a Story with Color

The paint palette on your computer has many different colors. How many different variations of one color can you find in your palette? Do you want to make a serious, calm, or sad picture? Make it in blues or greens. If your subject is cheery, think about using reds or orange-yellows.

Materials

- **Color printer, if available**
- **Computer printer paper**

1. Decide the color theme you would like to use in a painting. See how many variations of that color your paint palette offers.

2. Paint your entire picture using only variations of 1 color. View your masterpiece on-screen or print it, if you have a color printer. If you have a black-and-white printer, you can see how your picture looks in different shades of gray.

Colorful Crayons

How many variations of one color does your crayon box hold?
Try coloring the same picture different ways. One version may
use only different blues; another version may use only reds.

Materials

* **Computer printer paper**
* **Crayons**

1. Draw a picture in outline only; do not add color. Print 2 copies.

2. Color your first piece of artwork with blues. Look through your crayon box and pick out all the colors that are a type of blue. Use these crayons to add color to your line drawing.

3. Choose another color and repeat step 2 with the second copy.

4. Put the 2 pictures side by side. Do you get a different feeling from each color theme?

2. Colorful Characters

Artists always think about the colors they are using. Over the years artists have used color in very different ways. Changes happen because creative people like to try new things. Sometimes art styles change because of a new invention. There was a time in the history of art when both of these things happened. This is when color became king. To learn why it was an important time in painting, you need to know about the artists. Meet these colorful characters and try out some of their ideas on your own art.

Claude Monet

About 125 years ago, a group of French artists decided to shake up the art world. At the time, most artists painted pictures that looked as realistic and detailed as possible. Their brush strokes were very carefully done. These artists usually stayed indoors and painted in their studios. The colors they used were dark.

A young artist named Claude Monet (moh-NAY) and his artist friends were about to stir things up. They had the help of a new invention—it was the collapsible metal tube. Before the invention of the tube, artists had to carry their oil paints outside in a pig's bladder, but this wasn't too successful because the paint quickly dried up. However, with metal tubes of paint in his paint box, Monet could go outside and see the sun sparkling on the water. He wanted to capture the sunlight as it lit up the landscape. Monet painted in quick dabs of bright colors. The dabs became recognizable objects when you stood back to look at the picture.

Monet painted for a living. This meant that he had to sell his paintings. In France, the only way rich buyers could see an artist's work was at a place called the Salon. The Salon didn't let just anybody show their work. Paintings had to be judged by a jury of critics. This was a problem. The critics thought Monet's work was messy and unfinished, and the colors were so loud! The Salon refused to show his work.

It wasn't only Monet who was turned away. Other artists who painted in this freer, sunlit style had the same problems. The group decided to put on their own art show. One of the paintings that Monet exhibited was of a small boat on the water at sunrise. He titled it *Impression, Sunrise*. The art critics came to the show but did not like the paintings one bit. They decided to call this group of messy painters *Impressionists*. They didn't use this term as a compliment.

It took several years before people grew to love the work of the Impressionists. Eventually Monet made enough money to buy a home near Paris. He planted a beautiful garden and made a pond in it. Many of his paintings are of the water lilies that floated in this pond. He named his home Giverny (jee-ver-NAY).

Claude Monet
Water Lilies, 1914–15
$63\frac{1}{4}$ in. x $71\frac{6}{8}$ in.
Portland Art Museum, Portland Oregon

This detail from *Water Lilies* shows Monet's bold brushstrokes.

Impression, Water Lily

Create a picture in the style of the Impressionists. To do this you must see your subject the way they did—with a quick impression. You'll use one of Monet's favorite subjects: a water lily. Notice how the sun hits the petals, making bright highlights.

Materials

- Picture of water lily on previous page
- Computer printer paper
- Color printer, if available

1. Look at the photo of the lily in this book, while counting to 10. See the lily as colors and shapes, with dabs of light.

2. Close your eyes and see the lily in your mind. This is your impression of the lily.

3. Without looking at the photo again, paint your impression of the lily and include strokes and splashes of color to make the lily sparkle. Print out your lily, if you have a color printer.

Like Monet's paintings, your art probably won't look exactly like a lily. Stand across the room and look at your art. Does it look more like a lily now?

# Water Lily, Part 2

This is a great way to get the look of Monet's style. The melted crayons you use will give your picture a dreamy, impressionistic appearance.

Materials

- **Computer printer paper**
- **Microwave oven**
- **Dinner plate (microwaveable)**
- **Newspaper**
- **Crayons (required)**
- **You need an adult to help you with this activity.**

1. Draw a lily in outline only. Do not add color to it.

2. Print 1 copy.

3. Ask an adult to heat an empty dinner plate in the microwave set on high for 60 seconds.

4. When the timer goes off, the adult should place the plate on a table and cover it with a single layer of newspaper. The plate will be slightly warm to the touch.

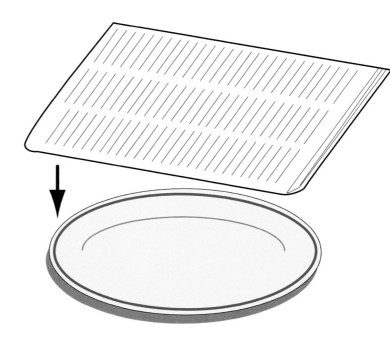

5. Carefully place your printed lily on top of the newspaper. Color the lily with crayons by slowly moving them across your picture as you press down. The crayons will make beautiful shapes on your picture as they melt. The colors will blend together, too.

You have to work fast because the crayons won't melt once the plate cools off.

Georges Seurat

If ever there was an artist who had patience, it was Georges Seurat (suh-RAH).

He was born in Paris in 1859 and entered art school when he was sixteen. As a student, he liked to visit art museums and study the paintings of the great Masters. He also spent a lot of his time at the library. He loved to read about the scientific discoveries that were being made about color. One of his favorite experiments was done by a physicist in Scotland named James Clerk Maxwell. Maxwell painted two colors on a disk. He discovered that they blended together when the disk was spun very rapidly. An American physicist, Ogden Rood, thought that you didn't have to spin a disk. Colors could seem blended just by painting small dots of two colors next to each other and looking at them from a distance. Because the colors were mixed in the eye, it was called *optical mixing*.

Seurat decided to paint entire pictures using small dots. Instead of mixing colors on his palette like other artists, he let the viewer's eye mix his tiny dots. His most famous painting was no small job. The picture he made was of a beautiful park scene. He called it *A Sunday on La Grande Jatte*. And it was grand! This huge canvas took up an entire wall. Seurat worked on it, dot by tiny dot, for two years until it was finished. He even painted a dotted frame around it. When you see this picture in person, the colors seem to sparkle and dance.

Other artists tried this style of painting, too. The only problem was that it took a very long time to paint a picture using tiny dots. Most artists didn't have the patience and went on to other styles. Painting with small dots, or points, is called *pointillism*.

Georges Seurat, French, 1859–1891
A Sunday on La Grande Jatte, 1884
Oil on canvas, 1884–1886, 207.5 cm x 308 cm
Helen Birch Bartlett Memorial Collection
Photograph ©1996, The Art Institute of Chicago

Seurat Goes Cyber

Paint a picture in Seurat's style by making dots of color on your screen. Notice how the different colors blend together when you look at them from across the room. Once you get the hang of dot drawing, add more things to the picture. You can add a stream, flower garden, or anything you'd like.

Materials

- **Computer printer paper**
- **Color printer, if available**
  or
- **Crayons**

1. Draw a simple outline of a tree.

2. Select the pencil tool. (If you are working with Kid Pix Studio, select the thickest line with rounded ends to paint little circles of color. If you are working with Paint or Paintbrush, select the paintbrush icon and the thickest line possible to paint little squares of color.) Set the color to green. Make green dots on the top of the tree for the leaves. You can do this by clicking the mouse many times while moving it around this space.

3. Change the color of your line to yellow and make a few dots of this color on the right side of the tree and its leaves. (It's OK to overlap the green dots a little.)

4. Change the color of your line to blue and make a few dots in the middle of the tree. Change the color to purple and make some dots on the left side of the tree.

5. Make the tree trunk with orange and brown dots.

6. Stand back and look at your masterpiece. It looks like your tree has sunlight shining on it from the right side. Finish the picture with dot art of your own.

7. Print a copy in color or black and white. If you have a black-and-white printer, your picture will be in shades of gray dots. Use crayons to make a colorful dotted frame around the picture.

Vincent van Gogh

Unlike most artists, Vincent van Gogh (van-GOH) didn't decide to become an artist until he was grown up. He was born in the Netherlands in 1853. As an adult, he wanted to be a preacher, like his father. He preached to very poor people who lived near the coal mines in Holland in the Netherlands. His early drawings were of these people. Life was very hard for them. The dark colors in van Gogh's early paintings help to show their sadness.

One day van Gogh decided to move to France to pursue his art. In Paris, he met Monet and other artists who were creating paintings using brighter colors. Van Gogh loved the idea of using bright colors. He decided to move to southern France, where the sun shone brightly over the beautiful countryside and the people were happy. This is where he painted his best pictures. Now his paintings were so bright, the colors almost screamed at each other. He liked to paint in complementary colors, using bright blues next to lively oranges and harsh reds next to brilliant greens. He knew that Seurat was mixing colors by using small dots of color. Van Gogh liked this idea, but instead of small dots he used swirling strokes and bold dabs of thick paint. Many of his paintings are of orange sunflowers or wheat fields against a bright blue sky. Van Gogh worked with a passion, and his colors show his excitement.

Vincent van Gogh
The Starry Night, 1889
Oil on canvas, 29 in. x $36\frac{1}{4}$ in.
The Museum of Modern Art, New York
Acquired through the Lillie P. Bliss Bequest
Photograph ©1997 The Museum of Modern Art, New York

Starry, Starry Night

Feel the swirls of Van Gogh's brush as you move to heavenly music. Make starry designs for your bedroom ceiling, or attach a star to the end of a straw to make a magic wand.

Materials

- **Radio playing relaxing music (maybe classical)**
- **Blue computer printer paper**
- **Orange and yellow puffy fabric paint**
- **Scissors**
- **Plastic drinking straw**
- **Masking tape**
- **Ribbon**

Let's Warm Up

Van Gogh used big, loose swirls when he painted the sky in *The Starry Night*. First, we'll practice these swirling motions. Listen to slow, dreamy music on the radio. Hold a straw in your hand and pretend you are conducting the music. Start by making big, sideways figure eights using your whole arm. Make swirls and circles, too. Next, try keeping your arm still and conduct by moving only your hand. This is how you'll draw Van Gogh's sky, using your mouse.

Let's Paint!

1. At your computer, use the pencil or brush tool to fill the screen with swirls. Make several kinds—some long and narrow, some smaller and round.

2. Print several copies on blue paper.

3. Squeeze fabric paint onto the first printed page to make halos and shimmers around the swirls. Do this on each of the printed pages. Let the paint dry.

4. Cut each page into the shape of one or more stars and tape them to your bedroom ceiling. Or, tape 1 star to one end of a plastic drinking straw to make a magic wand. You can add ribbons to the star on your wand to make it even more magical. Dance to dreamy music and swirl your wand through the air.

Sunflower Cereal Box

Start your day with a cheery breakfast à la Van Gogh. Keep your breakfast cereal in this beautiful container or use it to store sunflower seeds for your bird feeder.

Materials

- **3 pieces of yellow computer printer paper**
- **3 pieces of orange computer printer paper**
- **Scissors**
- **Newspaper**
- **1 oatmeal container (or other cylinder-shaped container), empty**
- **Blue poster paint**
- **Paintbrush**
- **Glue stick**

1. Draw a sunflower in black line only; do not add color. Make the center of the flower with a patterned fill. (If your drawing program doesn't have patterns, use your Seurat technique to draw tiny dots to fill up the center of each sunflower.)

2. Print 6 copies—3 on the yellow and 3 on the orange computer printer paper.

3. Cut out each flower and set aside.

4. Spread a sheet of newspaper on your work table. Paint the outside of the oatmeal box with blue paint. Let the paint dry.

5. Apply glue to the back of each cutout sunflower and press it onto the oatmeal box. Fill the container with your favorite cereal.

The Fauvists

In 1905, another style of painting shook up the art world, just when people were getting used to the Impressionists.

It all started at an art show that was known for introducing new artists. The exhibit was in Paris, France, in a large building that had several rooms. Many paintings were hung in each room. The show was a great success . . . until you came to room number seven. Room number seven held the brightest, most colorful paintings anyone had ever seen. And the colors didn't necessarily match what was painted. The face of a beautiful woman was painted in yellow and blue splotches. The green grass in a landscape was made with splashes of red, blue, and orange.

The colorful room caused quite a stir. Most people hated the artwork, saying "It's madness." Someone even tried to shred a canvas with a knife. One critic called it the work of wild beasts. In French, a wild beast is a *fauve* (fohv).

The Fauvists didn't want to make people angry with their art. They painted with bright colors to express their ideas. The Fauvists loved color, and they thought everyone else would, too. It took a few years for the public to see what they meant. Even the critics eventually agreed that the ideas of the Fauvists were a positive step in the history of art.

Something funny happened three years later at the same art show. By now the Fauvists were pretty popular. One of the judges for new entries that year was the most popular Fauvist of all. His name was Henri Matisse (mah-TEES). Matisse refused to allow a new type of painting style to be shown at the exhibit. To explain why he didn't like it, he took out a piece of paper and drew two interconnected cubes. "It was a canvas covered with little cubes," he said. Little did Matisse know then that these "little cubes" would be the next big art movement!

Colorful Critters

Ron Burns loves to paint in bright, imaginative colors. His idea of using color is much like that of the Fauvists. He doesn't mind one bit that his painting of Toby shows this puppy with pink ears and an orange-and-purple face or that in a piece called *Squirt* the kitten has bright yellow ears and a green-and-yellow tail. Ron has a whole series of colorful dogs and cats.

Ron Burns
Squirt, 1993
24 in. x 36 in.

Ron Burns
Toby, 1993
24 in. x 36 in.

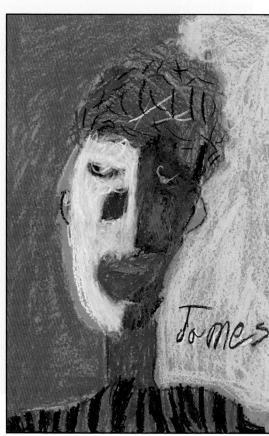

James Schaffer, age 7

Beauty and the Wild Beast

Paint your own portrait in the style of the Fauvists.

Materials

- **Mirror**
- **2 pieces of computer printer paper**
- **Color printer, if available**

  or

- **Crayons**

1. Place your mirror next to your computer, close enough so that you can see your reflection and your computer screen at the same time. Paint a realistic colorful portrait of yourself.

2. Save this file and call it "Beauty."

3. Change the colors on your first portrait. Match the style of the Fauvists by using bright, exaggerated colors. A green nose and purple hair would work just fine. Save this file as "Beast."

4. Print out both portraits. If you have a black-and-white printer, you can color with crayons right on top of the gray tones. Color one using naturalistic colors. Color the second one Fauvist-style using wild-colored crayons.

Introducing the Camera

The invention of the camera made a big impact on the art world. Painters no longer had to make their pictures look realistic. A camera could do that. Portrait painters made up one group that was really affected by this new invention. Previously, when wealthy people and royalty needed a likeness done, they hired a portrait artist. This was sometimes a hard job for the artist. Clients expected a beautiful likeness of themselves, even if they weren't so beautiful. Often the artist included things in the portrait that had meaning to the subject. For example, a young girl holding a pink carnation meant she was about to be married. If a woman was dressed in green it could mean she wanted to have children.

Camera pictures started taking the place of these painted portraits. Now the artists were free to express themselves in less realistic ways. This is one reason the Fauvists became so imaginative in their use of color.

Wild Beast Cookies

Decorate animal cookies and put them in the cookie jar you made on page 25. Or wrap them in plastic wrap, add a gift tag, and give them as a gift.

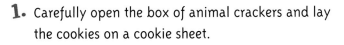

Materials

- **Box of animal crackers**
- **Cookie sheet**
- **Several colors of cake decorating icing tubes**
- **Ribbon and cookie tag or cookie jar from page 24 (optional)**

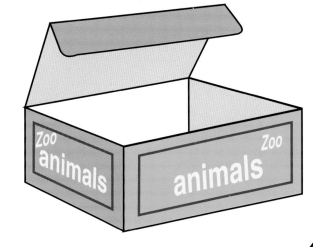

1. Carefully open the box of animal crackers and lay the cookies on a cookie sheet.

2. Decorate each cookie with bright squiggles of icing. Let the decorations dry, and put them in a cookie jar; or make the gift box in step 3.

3. Place the cookies back in their original box. Tie a ribbon around the box and make a bow. Tie one of the cookie company labels that you made on page 24 to the bow.

Henri Matisse

Henri Matisse (mah-TEES) almost didn't become an artist. He was born in France in 1869. When Matisse was twenty years old, appendicitis made him stay home from his job as a law clerk. His mother gave him a box of colored pencils to keep him occupied while he was recovering. He loved his gift! A year later, he quit his job and went to study art in Paris. Matisse learned a lot about drawing at art school. But he thought the instructors were too old-fashioned about painting with color. The "correct" way to paint, according to his teachers, was with a dark palette.

Matisse liked what Monet and the Impressionists were doing. He was also inspired by van Gogh's bright, complementary colors. Over the next few years, he used their ideas to create a style of his own. He wanted to use colors boldly, letting his imagination guide him. Other artists were experimenting with color, too. Together the group became known as the Fauvists and the movement was called Fauvism.

Throughout his life, Matisse painted in different styles. But in whatever he did, colors were bright and happiness was his message. Only once did he paint using grays and browns. It was during wartime and he was very worried that his son would be sent to fight. One of the paintings done at this time is of his son practicing the piano. The overall color is gray. It makes you sad when you look at it.

When Matisse was in his eighties, he was ill and had to stay in bed. He could no longer stand at his easel and paint. But this didn't stop him from creating! He began "painting" with colored paper. Using brightly colored sheets of paper, he cut out fanciful designs with scissors. The shapes were then glued to a background. In this way, Matisse designed stained glass windows, murals, and beautiful, bright pieces of art.

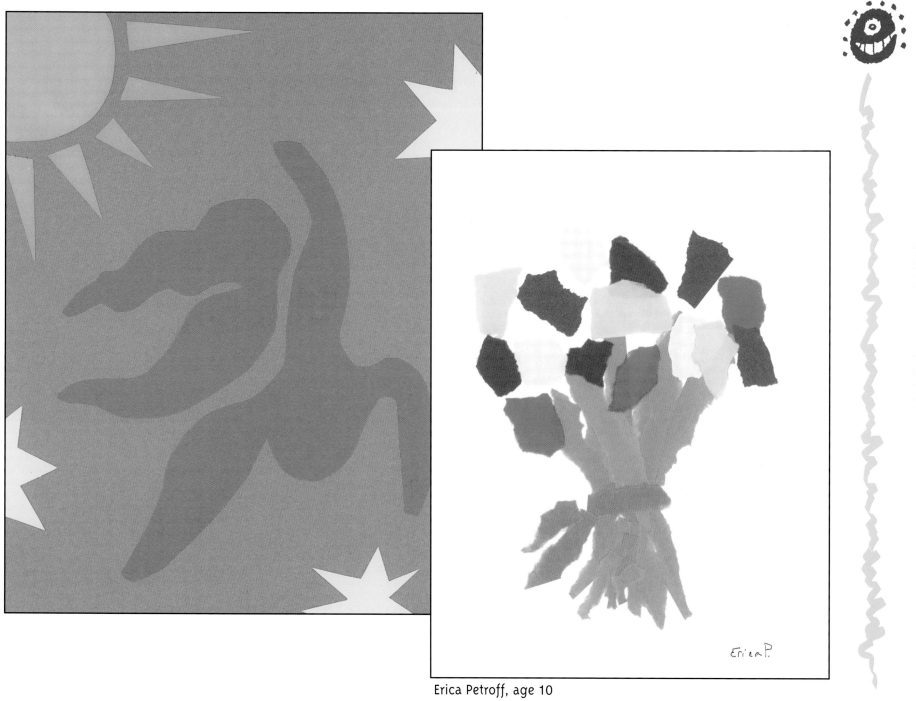

Erica Petroff, age 10

Matisse with Mouse

Matisse would have loved to see his designs lit up in bright colors on a computer. Unfortunately, it would be many years after his death before the first home computer was invented. But you can try out his style today when you make this birthday card.

Materials

- **Colored computer printer paper**
- **Scissors**
- **Glue stick**
- **Crayons**

4. Decide which colors you'd like to use for your birthday card. Put 1 piece of colored paper in the printer tray for each color in your design. Print as many copies as you have colors.

1. Draw a rectangle on the right half of your drawing area.

2. Inside the rectangle, draw the outline of a person.

3. Add a party hat and starbursts to the design. Be sure to make the outline of all these figures solid (so that the lines are not broken, to prevent the color from bleeding through). Keep your shapes simple.

5. Select the printed sheet that is to be the background. Fold it in half along its left edge with art facing out. Cut away excess paper.

6. Cut the shapes you need out of the remaining colors of paper. Glue these shapes onto the background color. Write a birthday message inside the card. Add small pieces of cut paper inside the card for confetti.

7. At your computer, add colors to your outline art. Save this file for your cyber gallery.

Pablo Picasso

Picasso was born in Spain in 1881. His father was an art teacher. As a young boy, Picasso had an incredible talent for drawing. Later he studied art at a famous school in Barcelona, Spain. But like many artists in those days, he moved to Paris to begin his career as a painter.

Picasso could paint perfect copies of the paintings of the old Masters. But he wanted to develop a style of his own. It took a few years to get established as an artist. At first he was lonely, hungry, and poor. It was at this time in his life that he painted pictures using mostly blues—his Blue Period. After a while he started making friends, and he even fell in love. He changed his palette to pink. This is called his Rose Period.

Picasso lived to be 91 years old. Throughout his life, he painted in many styles. His most famous style was one he developed with an artist friend, Georges Braque (brahk). The style is called *cubism*. Sometimes a cubist picture looks as if it's been broken into many pieces. Other times, it looks as though you are looking at the subject from many different viewpoints. A cubist picture of a woman may show part of her face looking right at you. In the same picture, part of the face will also be shown looking away. These two views are combined into one face.

Alfred Maurer
George Washington, 1932
39 in. x 24 in.
Portland Art Museum, Portland, Oregon

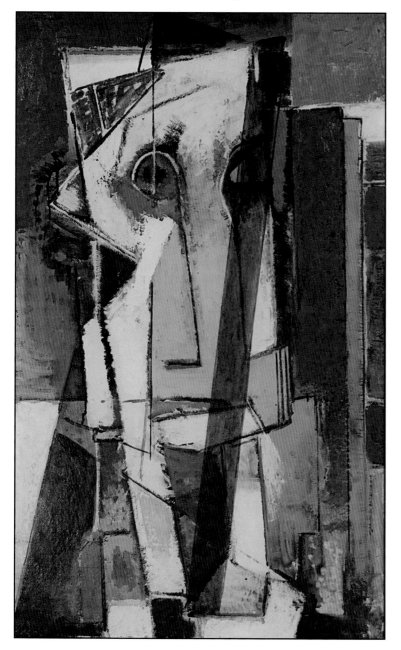

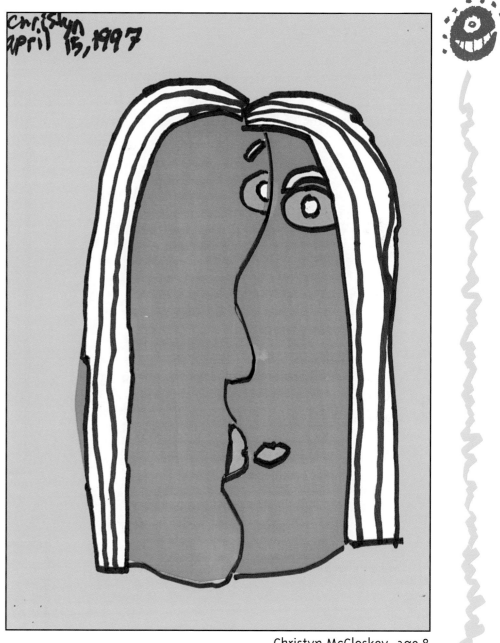

Christyn McCloskey, age 8

One of the things you notice about a cubist picture is that it is made up of many unusual shapes. The body of a person might be made of triangles, ovals, and squares. The shapes in this project can be made into anything you'd like. Just use your imagination.

Materials

- **1 piece of paper, 6 by 2 inches**
- **Pencil**
- **Clear plastic tape**
- **Computer printer paper**
- **Crayons**

1. On the piece of paper, draw 4 simple shapes such as a circle, square, triangle, and heart. Tape the piece of paper to the upper edge of your computer monitor, but do not cover your screen.

2. At your computer, use the pencil (or paintbrush) tool to draw one of the shapes anywhere on the screen. Be sure that your outline is solid (that the lines aren't broken and the shapes are closed completely).

3. Add a second shape that overlaps the first shape a little. Continue until you've drawn all 4 shapes, each shape overlapping another. Overlapping these shapes will give you many new shapes where these first 4 shapes overlap.

4. Use the paint bucket or paint roller tool to fill each shape with colorful solid fills.

5. Sit back and study your painting of crazy shapes. Imagine what kind of animal or object these shapes could look like if a few details, such as a tail, eyes, or ears, were added. Now you have your very own cubist creation.

6. Print 1 copy of your artwork. Use crayons to add color over the gray areas in the shapes.

Man in the Moon with Two Faces

A neat thing about cubist art is that the same subject can be drawn at different angles. For example, one part of a person's face could be looking at you. Another part could be drawn as if it were looking away. This activity lets you practice this technique by drawing a moon face. Once you get the hang of drawing this way, have fun drawing other faces in this style. Make a picture of someone you know.

Materials

- Computer printer paper
- 2 crayons: light yellow and light blue

2. Inside the circle, add a curved line in the shape of a quarter moon. Add in a nose and a mouth if you'd like.

1. Draw a large circle in the center of your screen.

Once in a Blue Moon

People say "once in a blue moon" when they mean something doesn't happen very often. There really is something called a blue moon, and it doesn't happen very often. Usually the moon is full only one time each month. But every so often there will be two full moons during one month. The second full moon is called a blue moon. The color of this moon isn't blue, though.

3. Draw an eye and a mouth on the quarter moon. Notice that this moon looks off to one side.

4. Draw an eye and a mouth on the rounded side of the circle. Notice that this full moon looks straight at you.

5. Print 1 copy of the picture.

6. Color the 2 faces in light tints of yellow and blue.

Wassily Kandinsky

Kandinsky (kan-DIHN-skee) was born in Moscow, Russia, in 1866. As an adult he studied law. But he was also interested in art. When he was thirty years old he turned down a job as a professor of law so that he could study painting. At that time, Munich, Germany, was a place full of new ideas about art. So Kandinsky moved to Munich, and a few years later he opened his own art school.

Kandinsky loved color! He believed that artists should use their imaginations when painting colors. He was also interested in music and thought art and music had many things in common. Music affects our feelings. Slow, soft music can make us sad. Fast, loud music makes us feel happy. He thought colors affected our feelings, too. Blue is soothing to us and yellow is exciting. Originally

Kandinsky called his paintings "color music." Many of his paintings are titled *Improvisation*. (The word *improvise* means to make something up as you go along and is usually used when talking about music.) By naming a piece improvisation, Kandinsky wanted to suggest that he let the colors take on shapes as he worked, without preplanning.

Kandinsky didn't think a picture had to look realistic. He let his message speak through different colored shapes. His style of painting didn't imitate nature and the world around him. Today we see many paintings that are done in this style. Some people believe that Kandinsky was the first artist to paint in this way, almost one hundred years ago.

Emil James Bisttram
Appassionato (Tone Poem), 1953
Enamel on masonite, 17 in. x 23$\frac{1}{2}$ in.
Gift of Edith Carlson O'Rourke
Utah Museum of Fine Arts

Imagination Station

Express your feelings with mouse-wiggles and paint splashes. Your picture shouldn't look like what you are thinking about. Just let the colors and shapes of your painting show your ideas.

Materials

- **Color printer, if available**
- **Computer printer paper**

1. Think of something that you did this week that made you excited or happy. Maybe you played soccer and kicked a great shot, or perhaps you sat under a tree and listened to a bird singing a beautiful song.

2. What colors come to mind when you think about this special time? An exciting game of soccer might make you think of red, or maybe you most remember the bright blue sky as you watched the ball flying. On the other hand, listening to a bird in a tree might make you think of the green, peaceful forest, or happy yellow chirps. Imagine your event in colors and shapes instead of actual objects.

3. At your computer, draw colorful shapes and lines to express your feelings about your special time.

4. Print out your creation and display it on your bedroom wall.

Georgia O'Keeffe

Georgia O'Keeffe was born in Wisconsin in 1887. She lived on a farm with her parents and six brothers and sisters. Even as a small child, O'Keeffe was interested in art. When she was twelve, her mother arranged for her to take drawing and painting lessons from an art teacher. Each Saturday she traveled seven miles in a buggy pulled by a horse to her art lesson.

O'Keeffe knew she wanted to be an artist. But one hundred years ago women did not usually become professional artists. But this didn't stop her. After high school, she was able to go to school at the Art Institute in Chicago. After learning the techniques of other artists, she worked to develop a style that was her own.

O'Keeffe wanted to show her new creations to someone, so she sent her artwork to a girlfriend in New York. She gave strict instructions not to show her work to anyone. However, her friend became so excited about the art that she ignored O'Keeffe's instructions. She took the work to a famous art gallery to show the owner. He loved them! He had them mounted and hung them in the best room of his gallery. When O'Keeffe found out, she was furious. But after she calmed down a bit she realized that it was an honor to have her work shown in this important gallery. She also noticed that her drawings were hung in the gallery's largest room. The work of two male artists was given space in smaller areas. Perhaps a woman *could* be a professional artist, she said. Years later, she married the owner of the gallery. He was a famous photographer. His name was Alfred Stieglitz (STEE-glitz).

O'Keeffe loved to paint flowers. Most people would paint a whole vase full of flowers. Georgia painted only one or two flowers in each picture. The flower would be much larger than real life. Imagine a poppy that's forty inches tall! You could look right into it, as if you were a bumblebee. She had a reason for making her flowers so large. She wanted even the busy New Yorkers to notice how beautiful a flower could be.

O'Keeffe loved color, too. She once said, "I found I could say things with color and shapes that I couldn't say in any other way—things I had no words for."

A Bee's Eye View

Draw a flower in the style of Georgia O'Keeffe and get a bee's eye view.

Materials

- 1 live flower
- Color printer, if available
- Computer printer paper
  or
- Colored computer printer paper
- Crayons

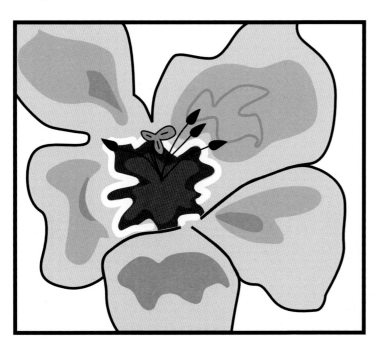

1. Pretend you are a bumblebee searching the garden for nectar. Carefully look at your flower. Hold it close to your eyes, close enough to see all its fine details. Look at it from all sides. What do you see when looking close-up that you never noticed before?

2. Decide what angle you want to paint your flower. Resting it on a table or on top of a little box, close to your eyes, will help you see its fine details.

3. Use the pencil or paintbrush tool on your painting program to draw this flower. Be sure to include your discoveries in your painting. It's OK if your artwork extends off the drawing area. This is how O'Keeffe drew her flowers.

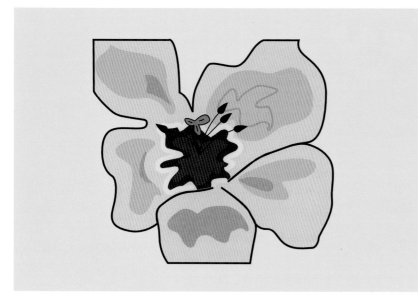

4. If you have a color printer, select colors from your paint palette that are the closest to their natural color, or, like many great artists, don't be restricted to what's found in nature. Paint the flower the colors that it makes you feel. Print a copy, hang it up, and enjoy.

5. If you have a black-and-white printer, try this: Change the colors in your flower so that they are all light shades of gray. Print your artwork on several sheets of colored paper. The light grays will show up, but they don't cover the color of the paper too much. Cut the flowers out and make a magical garden. You can also make 1 copy and use your crayons to color it.

Walt Disney

It all started with a little mouse.

Walter (better known to us as Walt) Disney was born in Chicago in 1901. Even as a small child, he liked to draw cartoons. Although he was a well-behaved student, young Disney was a problem to his teachers. While they stood at the chalkboard, Disney sat at his desk doodling. He wanted to become an artist.

Disney got his wish when he was eighteen years old. His first job in art was to make drawings for advertisements. Disney was always interested in new ideas. At the time he was beginning his career in art, a new type of moving cartoon was being invented. It was called *animation*. An animated cartoon is made up of many pictures that vary only slightly. Each picture is filmed and then played like a movie. Today everyone knows what a moving cartoon is, but back then it was an exciting new idea.

At first Disney thought he was too late to add anything new to the art of moving cartoons. Cartoonists in New York had been working on them already. But he decided that he could improve both the technology and the artistic quality of cartoons. He borrowed a camera and began experimenting with it in his garage. Soon he and another cartoonist started their own small business. His greatest success came when he drew a funny little mouse named Mickey.

Several new inventions helped Disney become a leader in the art of animation. At the time moving cartoons were first invented, regular movies had no sound. In 1927 the first motion picture with sound, *The Jazz Singer*, was made. Some people thought that sound pictures were just a passing fad. But Disney knew sound was the wave of the future. At last, Mickey would talk! His first talking cartoon was called *Steamboat Willie*. Disney's voice was the sound of Mickey. The cartoon was a smash.

People loved to watch animated films, but up until then films were only black and white. Four years after his first "talkie," Disney learned about a new invention. It was a film process called Technicolor. It allowed motion pictures to have color. But regular paint wouldn't work on the cartoon artwork. Disney and his lab technicians worked night and day to develop new paints. They invented paints that would stick to the illustrated artwork and not fade under hot lights. Disney was the first artist to make a color animated cartoon. That year, the film won an Oscar. It was the first time a cartoon had ever won.

Twirling Lollipop Cartoon

This cartoon looks like a lollipop. It will do magical things when you give it a twirl. Try making other cartoons, too. Make a bird in its cage. Try a "blinky" face with eyes that open and close.

Materials

- **Computer printer paper**
- **Scissors**
- **Crayons**
- **Clear plastic tape**
- **Plastic drinking straw**

1. Use the oval shape tool in your computer drawing program to create a 2-inch circle. Copy this circle and paste a second circle on the page.

2. Use the pencil or paintbrush tool to draw the outline of a fishbowl inside one of the circles. Make the bowl as large as you can.

3. Draw a goldfish inside the other circle.

4. Print a copy and cut out each circle.

5. Color the art.

6. Tape the back of 1 circle to the end of a straw. Turn the art face down and tape the other circle to the other side of the straw. *Hint—Use a rolled piece of tape that is sticky on both sides to secure the circle.*

7. Hold the straw between your 2 palms, with your arms stretched out in front of you. Move your hands back and forth to make the artwork twirl. Look at the goldfish as you twirl the stick. It should look like the fish is inside the fishbowl!

Dancing Pixels

If you have a Macintosh computer, you can make a moving cartoon by using Scrapbook. Practice making a dancing stick figure. After you get the hang of it, make cartoons of your own. You can add colors, too.

Materials

- **Macintosh computer with the Scrapbook accessory**
- **Ruler**

Making the Cartoon Frames

1. Draw a 4-inch-wide by 3-inch-tall rectangle on $\frac{1}{2}$ of your drawing area. Inside the rectangle, draw a stick figure.

2. Copy the first rectangle and stick man. Paste a duplicate onto the other side of your computer screen.

3. Erase the second figure's arms and legs and redraw them, making slight changes in the position of its arms and legs.

Placing the Cartoons in Macintosh Scrapbook

1. Select the first rectangle and stick man. Go to the Edit menu and make a copy. Go to the Apple menu and select Scrapbook. Go to the Edit menu and select the Paste command. Now you have pasted 1 frame of your cartoon into the Scrapbook. Close the Scrapbook.

2. Select the second rectangle and stick man. Repeat step 1, starting with "Go to the Edit menu" and make a copy. You've made the second frame of the cartoon.

3. Repeat steps 1 and 2, alternating the drawings, until you have about 6 frames.

4. To view your cartoon, open the Scrapbook and hold down the right or left arrows of the scroll bar. The stick man will seem to be dancing, as the frames of the Scrapbook change.

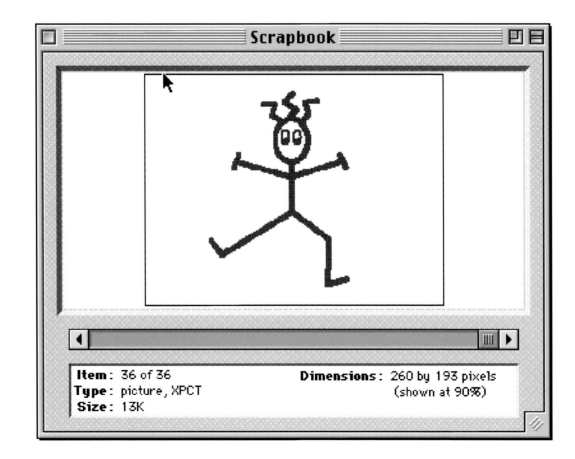

Bad Hair Day

Make a type of cartoon called a flip book. You can draw a small flip book on your computer.

Materials

Materials

- **Ruler**
- **Computer printer paper**
- **Scissors**
- **Crayons**
- **Stapler**

1. Draw a 4-inch wide by 3-inch-tall rectangle on your computer screen. Copy and paste about 15 duplicates. You might need extra drawing pages to fit all the rectangles.

2. Draw 1 frame of your cartoon—a simple picture of anything such as a flower with its petals falling or a waste basket filling up with trash—in each rectangle. In our example, we've created a figure with bad hair. The facial expression and hair change a little in every frame.

Hint—Copy the last frame you've drawn and paste it into the next frame. Then change this picture a little.

Bad Hair Day!

3. Print 1 copy and cut out each rectangle.

4. If you printed in black and white, add color with crayons.

5. Stack the rectangles in their correct order and staple 1 edge.

6. Flip through the pages of your book to see your artwork come to life.

3. Mother Nature's Paintbrush

Of all the painters, Mother Nature is by far the most colorful. Nature's bright colors and exciting patterns have been copied by artists since the days of the cave dwellers. Artists use many paints that come from nature's bright berries and colorful minerals.

Just like an artist, Mother Nature usually has a purpose for using colors the way she does. Some birds and insects look like they were painted by the Fauvists. They show off in their brightly colored outfits to attract mates or to say "This spot is mine." Other animals wear a disguise called camouflage (CAM-a-flaj). They are colored to match their living quarters. Critters that are colored in camouflage can hide from things that would like to eat them. Or, they can sit still until an unsuspecting meal walks across their path. Then there are the insects and frogs that are so bright they couldn't be missed.

It doesn't take long for others to know that these creatures taste bad and will give them a stomachache. That's only if the unfortunate eaters live to remember their mistake. These morsels can be poisonous.

Nature's colorful palette doesn't stop with the animal kingdom. Her flower gardens and coral reefs have every color imaginable. Even though we enjoy a beautiful garden, the flowers are really colored to attract birds and insects. These are the busy helpers that pollinate the flowers and spread their seeds so that more flowers can sprout. Some insects, such as bees, can see colors that we can't. Their eyes allow them to see another hue called ultraviolet. What we see as a white or yellow flower may look like purple to them. This helps them find exactly the right flower to visit.

Colorful Warnings

It's a jungle out there! Insects and amphibians spend a lot of their time just trying to avoid being eaten. Some critters are fast, while others are good at hiding. Some critters use color as a way of saying "Eat me and you'll be sorry." Insects and amphibians in this poisonous group are usually colored bright red, yellow, or orange. Often they'll have black patterns on them, too.

The monarch butterfly is so beautiful, you'd never think it was so dangerous. Monarchs become poisonous because as caterpillars they eat milkweed plants. The poison from the milkweed doesn't harm the monarch caterpillar, but it will harm other insects.

Young birds quickly learn that a monarch nibble tastes terrible. Birds, who can see color very well, learn that this orange-and-black butterfly is something to be left alone.

The monarch has a twin that is not poisonous at all. This butterfly is called a viceroy. The viceroy is a little smaller, but exactly the same color as the monarch. Because birds learn to avoid orange and black, they leave the tasty viceroys alone.

Some frogs and toads, such as the Strawberry Poison-Dart Frog and Red-Bandit Crevice Creeper, also use color to warn others to stay away. They are usually colored red, orange, or yellow. Their poison is stored in glands under their skin.

Monarch Butterfly Magnet

This butterfly can hold notes to your refrigerator door or perch on a metal desk lamp.

Materials

- **Orange computer printer paper**
- **Scissors**
- **Vinyl magnet**
- **Glue stick**
- **Chenille stem**
- **Clear plastic tape**

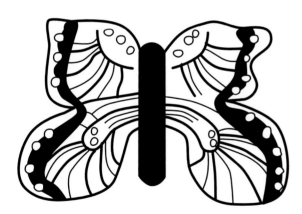

1. Draw the outline of a butterfly.

2. Add the patterns of a monarch's wings in black. Print 1 copy on orange paper.

3. Cut out the butterfly shape.

4. Cut a long, narrow piece from a vinyl refrigerator magnet. Glue it to the underside of the butterfly's body. Tape 2 pieces of chenille stem for the antennas at the butterfly's head.

Bathtub Buddy

Brave a bath with a poisonous pal that you've made yourself. He can float in the tub or stick to the bathtub wall. Make some for your friends and play with them in your swimming pool.

Materials

- **Orange, yellow, or red computer printer paper**
- **Scissors**
- **Newspaper**
- **Pencil sharpener**
- **Black crayon (required)**
- **Clothes iron**
- **Clear sticky laminate paper**
- **You need an adult to help you with this activity.**

1. Draw an outline of a leaping frog. Print 1 copy.

2. Cut out the frog shape. Fold the shape in half down the center of its back.

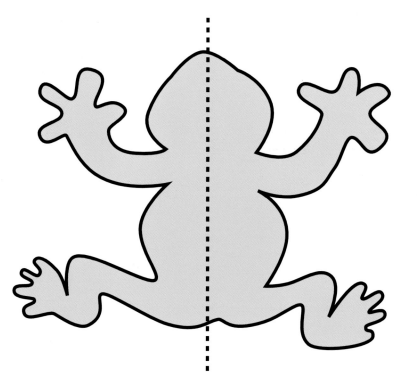

3. Cover your work area with newspaper. Unfold the frog and place it on top of the newspaper.

4. Use a pencil sharpener to make a small pile of black crayon shavings. Sprinkle the shavings on one half of the frog. Fold the frog along the original crease and place 1 sheet of newspaper over the frog that has the crayon shavings inside.

Bathtub Buddy (continued)

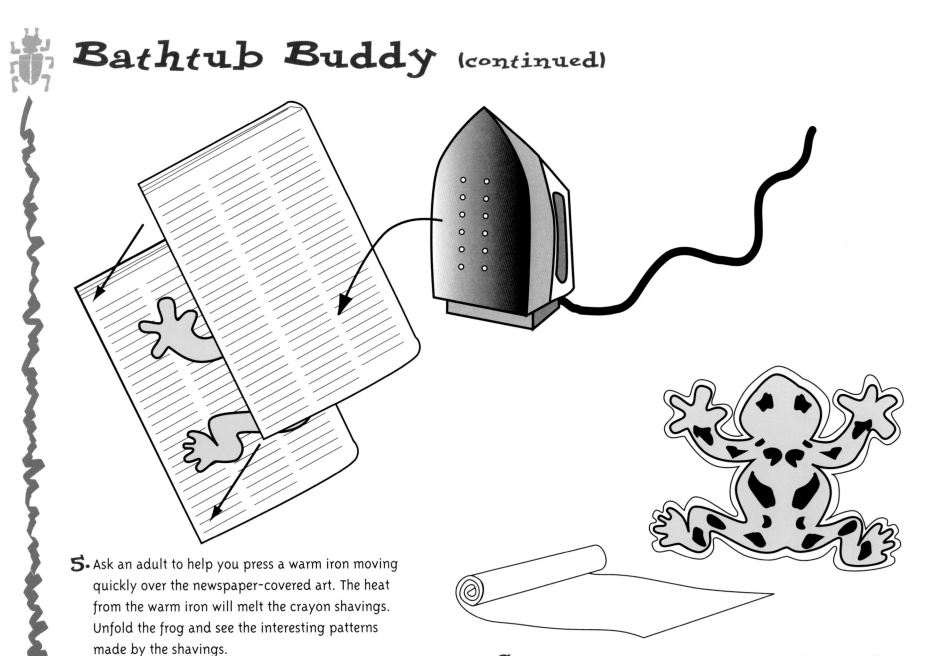

5. Ask an adult to help you press a warm iron moving quickly over the newspaper-covered art. The heat from the warm iron will melt the crayon shavings. Unfold the frog and see the interesting patterns made by the shavings.

6. Cut 2 pieces of clear laminate paper that are a little larger than the frog. Apply 1 sheet of clear sticky laminate paper to each side of the frog. Trim it close to the outline of the frog's shape.

Another animal that can be pretty potent is the skunk. Anyone who has smelled a skunk's aroma knows to keep out of his way. But skunks aren't colorful. That's because they are *nocturnal* (nok-TURN-al). Nocturnal animals sleep during the day and come out after dark. Colors can't be seen in the dark, but a white stripe down the back of a black skunk can be seen very easily. Animals that are nocturnal use black and white for their colorful warnings.

Nature-Inspired Art

Many things in nature have beautiful patterns. Artists are often inspired by these beautiful colors and designs.

Tapestry Art

Nancy Smith Klos is an artist who "paints" with colors of yarn. She uses what she learned about color and light—when she trained to be a painter—in her weavings. The pieces of yarn are woven into a picture using a loom. This type of art is called tapestry weaving. Klos's love of nature shows in her work. She gets many of her ideas from the colors and patterns of nature. This colorful design was inspired by the beautiful patterns on the wings of monarch butterflies. The monarchs are clustering together in a tree during their migration. Can you see the different butterflies?

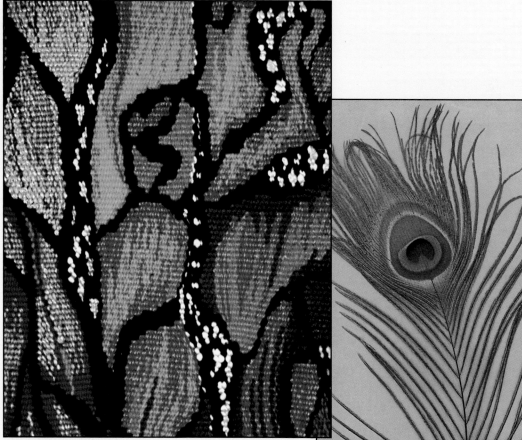

Nancy Smith Klos
Monarch Cluster (detail)
Woven miniature tapestry,
12 in. x 12 in.

Colors from Nature

Let a picture of a peacock feather be the inspiration for your next masterpiece. Be on the lookout for other things in nature that would make colorful designs. The pattern of a butterfly's wing or spots on a leopard are just a few of the many choices.

Materials

- **Real peacock feather or picture from this book**
- **Computer printer paper**
- **Crayons**

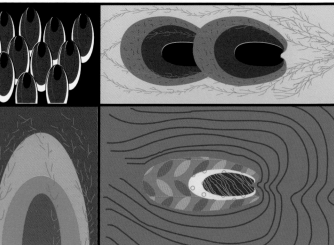

1. Study the peacock feather to see what type of patterns it has. Notice all its colors.

2. At the computer, draw a line across the screen (horizontal) in the middle. Draw another line up and down (vertical) in the middle. This divides the drawing area into 4 sections. (They don't have to be the exact same size.)

3. In 1 section, draw 1 pattern that you can see on the feather. Make this pattern big and close-up; don't draw the whole feather. Color the pattern with the colors you find in the feather, or use interesting pattern fills (if available on your program) to suggest a color.

4. Repeat step 3 in the remaining 3 sections of your computer screen, but draw a different pattern in each section.

5. Print out your artwork. Even if you have a black-and-white printer, the designs will be beautiful. Add a colorful border with crayons. Use all the colors you see in the peacock feather.

Colorful Disguises

Another way animals stay safe is by blending into their environment (where they live). Sometimes this means having the drab colors of twigs and dried leaves. Baby birds are often born with colors that match their nest. When they hatch from their egg, they can't fly or even see. By blending into their home, they can stay safe.

Other birds look very colorful but also blend into their environment. A bright green-and-yellow parrot really stands out when you see it at a pet store. If you saw it in the rain forest where it lives, it would blend into the bright green leaves and patches of yellow sunshine.

A coral reef is the most colorful place on earth. The fish who live in the reef are just as colorful. (If you don't want to become someone's dinner, it's best to match the colors of the reef.) Another way some fish fool their predators is with patterns called false *eyespots*. An eyespot is a decoration on the fish's fin that looks like an eye. A hungry fish who nibbles at this spot gets a mouthful of fin as its prey swims away.

Fish that live in the deep open ocean have duller colors. Those that live near the surface of the water have *countershading*. This means the fish has a light-colored belly and a dark-colored back. Countershading helps the fish hide when there is nowhere to hide. A bird flying overhead will not notice the fish because it blends into the dark water. But to a bigger fish swimming below, its light underside blends in with the sun shining overhead. Many birds have countershading, too.

Find the Fish

Practice designing camouflage by creating your own type of colorful fish.

Materials

- Computer printer paper
- Scissors
- 1 large sheet of wrapping paper with a colorful design
- Crayons

1. Draw a large outline of a fish.

2. Decorate the fish with lines, circles, stripes, and shapes. Do not add color to your artwork. Print 2 copies.

3. Cut out the fish shapes.

4. Place the piece of wrapping paper on your work table. Lay 1 of the fish cutouts over the wrapping paper.

5. Choose crayon colors that match the colors in the wrapping paper. Color the fish. If this were a real fish living in this environment, it would be able to hide because it is camouflaged.

6. Lay the second fish cutout over the wrapping paper. Choose crayon colors that are **not** in the wrapping paper design. Use these to color this fish. These colors make this fish stand out from the wrapping paper. If this were a real fish, and it stood out this much, it would be a very nervous fish!

Magical Aquarium

Coral reef under the sea are very colorful and beautiful. Make your own colorful reef aquarium with the wrapping paper you used in the project on page 106. You'll have a place for your fish to live. Draw other sea creatures on your computer and place them in your aquarium, too.

Materials

- **Large sheet of wrapping paper and camouflaged fish from the project on page 106**
- **Shoe box**
- **Pencil**
- **Scissors**
- **Glue stick**
- **Ruler**
- **Thread**
- **Clear plastic tape**
- **Computer printer paper**

1. Lay the piece of wrapping paper, design-side down, on top of a table. Place the shoe box, face up, on top of the piece of wrapping paper. Use a pencil to draw an outline around the box's bottom.

2. Cut out this shape.

3. Stand the box up on 1 of its sides. Again, trace around the outer edge of the box with a pencil.

4. Cut this shape out. Repeat this process for all of the sides of the box. Once finished, you should have 5 pieces of cut wrapping paper.

5. Apply glue to the inside bottom of the box. Place the piece of wrapping paper that fits this area into the box, face up, and press down.

6. Repeat this process for the remaining 4 sides of the box. Set the box on 1 side so that you can look into it. This is your coral reef.

7. Cut a 4-inch length of thread. Tape one end of the thread onto the top edge of the fish that matches this habitat. Tape the other end to the inside (or ceiling) of the shoe box.

8. Draw other sea creatures on your computer. Print them. Cut them out and place them inside your aquarium.

Underwater Colors

Have you ever noticed how distant scenery seems faded? A mountain covered with green trees looks pale and washed out when it's far away. Something happens to colors seen underwater, too. The deeper they are, the more they fade away. If you were to scuba dive down deep in the ocean, you wouldn't be able to see the beautiful colors in the reef. The color red fades first and appears dark or black. Yellow lasts deeper down, but it appears greenish. The color blue is seen deepest underwater. Because bright reds and oranges fade, most animals living deep down in the ocean are colored dull brown, green, and blue.

Design a Habitat

Cut out a picture of a critter from a magazine.
Use your computer to design a safe home for it.

Materials

- **Magazines with animal or insect pictures**
- **Scissors**
- **Clear plastic tape**
- **Color printer, if available**
- **Computer printer paper**

1. Look through a magazine to find an interesting critter. It can be an insect, fish, or anything you'd like. Cut it out *after* you get permission. Be sure to cut close to the animal so that no background shows.

2. At your computer, tape your animal onto the monitor. Notice how the animal stands out against the white drawing area. Paint a background on your page that the animal will blend into, so it can hide. You're designing a habitat.

3. Stand back from your monitor to test out your design. See if the animal is hidden by the colors you've painted.

4. If you have a color printer, print a copy of your design. See if the animal blends in with the printed page.

Strange as it may seem, a zebra's flashy coat helps hide it. Lions look for animal shapes when hunting for their next meal. Because the zebra's stripes go up and down, its shape is harder to see. To a hungry lion, a distant herd of zebras can look like a confusing mass of stripes. If a zebra's stripes went sideways, it would stand out more easily because it would still look horse-shaped.

Can All Animals See Colors?

Animals have such different eyes! Some, like hawks, can see better than we can. On the other hand, worms can just tell the difference between light and dark. And remember, some animals have fake eyespots (like fish). This confuses predators who can't tell which way its possible meal is looking or watching.

Animals live in such different places, it's not surprising that they have different types of eyes. You would be surprised where some of these eyes are found. A starfish has eyes at the tips of its arms. Snails and crabs have them at the ends of stalks above their heads. These move around, giving these creatures a wide range of view. Lobsters have light-sensitive areas on their tails. This helps let them know when they're being chased.

Different types of eyes see differently. Most animals don't have color vision comparable to ours. Dogs, cats, and horses have poor color vision. Even though they can't see all colors, they enjoy other advantages; for example, a cat can see better in the dark than we can.

Insects see some of the colors we see, and they see some that we can't. Snakes go even further. They have receptors to detect (almost "seeing") heat. In the darkest night, they can chase a mouse by following the heat from its body.

Birds have great eyesight. Hunters like hawks and eagles can clearly see a distant mouse. And owls can see in very dim light. Birds may see colors differently than we do. They can see colors that are invisible to us. Scientists think birds can even see the sun on a cloudy day. This helps the birds know where they are on their long migrations.

You Are What You Eat

Flamingos are pink because of what they eat. They get their coloring from the small shrimp-like animals they eat that provides them with beta-carotene. This turns their new feathers pink. There are several species of flamingos, and some get pinker than others (not because they eat more than the others). What color would you be if you were the color of your favorite food?

Leonardo da Doggy

What if your dog or cat could paint? It wouldn't be very colorful because they can't see all of the colors that we can. This project shows you how your pet might see the world.

Materials

- **Computer printer paper**

1. Draw a picture of your dog or cat. Try to match all the colors that you see.

2. Print 1 copy of your picture. If you have a color printer, set it to print only in grayscale and then print your 1 copy.

3. Look at the printed picture. All of the colors you painted were changed to a shade of gray. This is how many animals see the world.

Making Colors from Nature

When it's time to paint in art class, paint jars and brushes are waiting for you. All you have to do is open the jars and start painting. It wasn't always so easy, and many of the famous artists whose work you see in museums had to prepare their paints by themselves. That's a lot of work!

The earliest paints were made from natural materials in the earth. By grinding up different minerals, early artists could make red, yellow, and brown colors. A good black was made from charcoal, and ground up snail shells made blue! This color was so popular that the snail was almost wiped out. Another blue, called ultramarine, was made from crushed stone mined in Afghanistan. It's called ultramarine because it came from across the ocean. This color was so expensive it was used only for special occasions.

Other colors were made from plants. The roots, leaves, and sap could be turned into colors. In early Mexico, even insects were put to good use. Most amazing of all, ground up mummies were found to make a perfectly good brown color. It was called mummy brown. The most expensive color of all was made from gold. Gold could be made into very thin sheets (gold leaf) and applied to a wooden background. Religious pictures used gold for special effects.

In the American Southwest, colored sands are used by Native Americans for sand paintings. Rocks of different colors are collected, even if it means climbing up a steep cliff and hammering away. The rock is crushed and made into beautiful designs. Colors made from vegetables are used to decorate the beautiful pottery made by Native Americans, too.

A Passion for Purple

Sometimes accidents work out better than you might think. In the 1850s, a purple dye was discovered accidentally by an eighteen-year-old chemistry student named William Henry Perkin. He was trying to make a substitute for quinine, a medicine that battled malaria a disease that was killing thousands of people every year.

While the student mixed his chemicals, he discovered a purple-colored substance. He thought it could be used as a dye for fabrics. After getting his father and older brother interested in his invention, Perkin convinced them to invest their life savings to finance the production of this new dye.

At first, when the young inventor tried to sell it, some artists didn't like it. Others, like artists in France, loved the new color. They named it *mauve* (mov). Eventually, it became such a success that Perkin retired at age 35, a very wealthy man.

Spicy Bookmark

Design a bookmark on your computer. Color it with crayons and curry powder yellow. You'll make your own paint, like artists did long ago.

Materials

- **Ruler**
- **Computer printer paper**
- **Crayons**
- **Curry powder paint (see recipe on page 117)**
- **Paintbrush**
- **Scissors**
- **Glue stick**
- **Hole puncher or pencil**
- **Yarn**

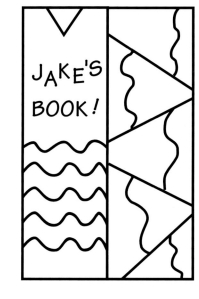

1. Draw a 4-inch-wide by 6-inch-high rectangle. Make a line down the center to divide the width into two 2-inch halves. Each half will be one side of the bookmark.

2. Make designs or type words on each half of the bookmark. Print 1 copy in black only.

3. Color the bookmark with crayons and curry powder paint.

4. Cut the rectangle from the printed page. Apply glue to the back of the artwork and fold it in half with the designs facing out. Press the folded paper so that the front and back stick together. Punch a hole in the top of the bookmark, thread a 4-inch piece of yarn through this hole, and gently tie it.

Now you're ready to get your favorite book and sit down and read! Don't worry if you can't finish the book in one sitting. You have a wonderful bookmark to hold your place.

Curry Powder Paint

Make a beautiful shade of yellow using something from Mother Nature's spice rack. Curry powder is actually made up of several ground herbs and spices.

Materials

- **Curry powder**
- **Water**
- **$\frac{1}{2}$ teaspoon measuring spoon**
- **Spoon**
- **Small bowl**

1. In a bowl, mix $\frac{1}{2}$ teaspoon of curry powder with $\frac{1}{2}$ teaspoon of water.

2. Mix it until it's a watery paste. Paint away!

4. Colorful Discoveries

There are many ways to explore color with your computer. Some of these require extra equipment, like a CD-ROM disc drive or an Internet connection. If you already have these things on your computer, you can do the activities in this chapter right away. If you don't have these things at home, ask your school or library if they do. However, you can still make the projects in this section even if you don't have access to the Internet. Look for suggestions with each activity.

Then again, there's always the old-fashioned way to explore. The best way to study the world of color is by being a part of the world. There's nothing like seeing the pink feathers of a flamingo at the zoo or Monet's pink water lilies at an art museum. What's more colorful than a walk in a beautiful garden? There are so many ways to learn more about this colorful world.

Internet Exploring

You can learn more about famous paintings by visiting an art museum. If you have an Internet connection on your computer, you won't even have to put on your shoes. The Internet connects your computer to others all around the world. If someone wants you to visit them on the Internet, they create a Web page.

Many art museums have a place on the Internet where you can see their paintings. Drop in on the Louvre in Paris, or take a cyber stroll through the Cleveland Museum of Art. Maybe the museum near you has a Web page, too. Call them on the phone and ask for their Web site address. It would be fun to study about a painting on your computer. Then you can visit the real museum to see what the painting looks like in person.

Another way to explore a museum is with an art *CD-ROM*. A CD-ROM is a computer disc that can contain pictures, sounds, and videos. Your computer must have a CD-ROM disc player to be able to use this type of software. Some museums have put together CD-ROMs with pictures from their art collections. The CD-ROM might even have a short movie about an artist or an artsy game to play. You can find CD-ROMs at stores that sell computers. Many libraries have art CD-ROMs that you can check out, too.

Web Sites for Colorful Discoveries

Here are a few Web site addresses to get you started on a colorful tour in cyberspace. Many art museums, zoos, and aquariums have Web pages to visit. Remember to carefully type each address exactly as it appears here. The Internet is not very forgiving when it comes to typing mistakes.

WebMuseum, Paris
http://watt.emf.net/

National Gallery of Art, Washington, D.C.
http://www.nga.gov/

Cleveland Museum of Art
http://www.clemusart.com/

Los Angeles County Museum of Art
http://www.lacma.org/

Zoo Atlanta
http://www.zooatlanta.org/

Monterey Bay Aquarium
http://www.mbayaq.org/

Mona Lisa and Me

One of the most famous paintings in the world is the Mona Lisa. This painting by Leonardo da Vinci hangs in the Louvre, in Paris. You can visit the WebMuseum, Paris, and bring the Mona Lisa home. It's easy on the Internet. Just dial up a cyber museum. Once you've drawn your own version of the Mona Lisa, explore other famous paintings. The home page of this Web site can be found at:

http://watt.emf.net/

Materials

- **Internet connection**
- **Computer printer paper**
- **Crayons**

Without the Internet:

If you don't have an Internet connection, skip steps 1 through 6 and go to the library. A good place to find a picture of the Mona Lisa is in a book about Leonardo da Vinci. You can tape a copy of this image on the side of your computer screen in step 7.

1. Log onto the Internet and type in this address: http://watt.emf.net/

2. Click on "Famous Paintings."

3. Click on "Artist Index."

4. Click on "Leonardo da Vinci."

5. Click on "Mona Lisa."

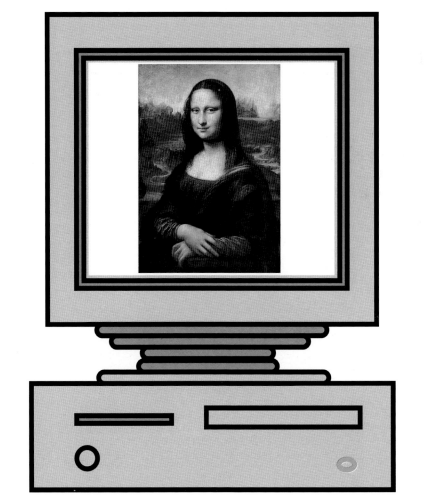

6. With your mouse, point to the picture of the Mona Lisa. Press down on the picture and choose the command "Copy Image" or "Copy." (The menu choices may be a bit different depending on which Internet software you're using, but they are very similar.) If you'd like to see a larger picture, hold down on the picture and drag to the command "Open Link." Log off from the Internet when you're through.

7. Open your paint or drawing program. Go to the Edit menu to paste the picture of the Mona Lisa. Place it to 1 side of the screen. Use the other side of the screen to paint your own version of this famous painting.

Leonardo da Vinci, 1452–1519
Mona Lisa, 1513–1519
Courtesy of Wood River Gallery

8. Select the real picture of the Mona Lisa and delete it. Print 1 copy of your own artwork.

9. Use crayons to draw a fancy frame around your masterpiece.

Sea Garden

Surfing at the Aquarium

Take a swim without getting wet. Once you visit an aquarium on the Internet, you'll want to meet these fishy friends in person. In computer lingo, *surfing* means exploring. Explore the Monterey Bay Aquarium site at:

http://www.mbayaq.org/

You can visit the amazing kelp forest. It'll inspire you to make a sea garden of colorful creatures. If you don't have an Internet connection, skip steps 1 and 2. Explore life in the kelp forest in books about marine life.

Materials

- **Internet connection**
- **Crayons, color computer printer paper, or color printer**
- **Scissors**
- **Clear plastic tape**
- **Green ribbon, white ribbon (optional)**
- **Plastic drinking straw**
- **Ruler**

1. Log on to the Internet and type this address: http://www.mbayaq.org/

2. Take time to explore this Web site. Look at the pictures of interesting fish and sea life. Read about life in a kelp forest. You can even find out what the scientists at the aquarium are researching.

3. Log off the Internet and open your computer paint or drawing program. Draw some of your favorite sea creatures.

4. Color your sea critters on-screen if you have a color printer. If you have a black-and-white printer, add color with crayons, or print the art on colored paper.

5. Cut out each shape.

6. Tape 3 long green pieces of ribbon to the straw, 1 on each end and 1 in the middle. Tape your sea art to the ribbons. If you made a jelly fish, add white ribbons for tentacles.

7. Cut a 15-inch piece of ribbon and tie 1 end of the ribbon to each end of the straw. Now you're ready to hang your sea creatures from the ceiling (with an adult's help) or on a doorknob or bedpost.

Send an E-mail Masterpiece

No more boring E-mail! If you have E-mail hooked up to your computer, you can send a picture along with your letter. Grandma can see your latest creations with the click of a button. Don't forget about cyber birthday cards. Your friends will love opening a letter that has one of your paintings attached. (Note: To be able to see the picture, the person you send a picture to in some cases will need to have the same software paint program as you have. She'll need to have an E-mail connection, too.)

Materials

- **E-mail hookup**
- **E-mail address of a friend**

1. Make a piece of art in a computer paint program. Draw a picture if you're inspired, or draw a lot of shapes, depending on your mood. Save your file and be sure to remember the name you give it.

2. Log on to the Internet and open the E-mail function.

Helpful Hint—If you're using Kid Pix Studio, draw your E-mail artwork in the Moopies or Stampimator program. You can then save your art under "Save as Stand Alone" in the File menu. If you do this, the person who receives your letter will not need Kid Pix software on his computer. He will be able to see your picture without it.

3. Type in your friend's E-mail address. Type a message if you want.

4. Look on your E-mail page for a function that says "Attach File." Click on this function. A menu will come up that allows you to find the name of your artwork. Click on your artwork file name. By doing this, your art file will be sent along with your message.

Hint—Include a PS in your letter to tell your friend to open the attached file.

If you don't have E-mail, you can still send a homemade card. To turn your piece of art into a postcard, just glue it to a piece of poster board. Write a message on the left side of the back side and write the address on the right side. Place a stamp in the top right corner and you're ready to send your homemade masterpiece by good old snail mail.

E-mail the Author

It would be great to get an E-mail letter from you. Send one of your creations along with your message. My address is: Sabbeth@aol.com

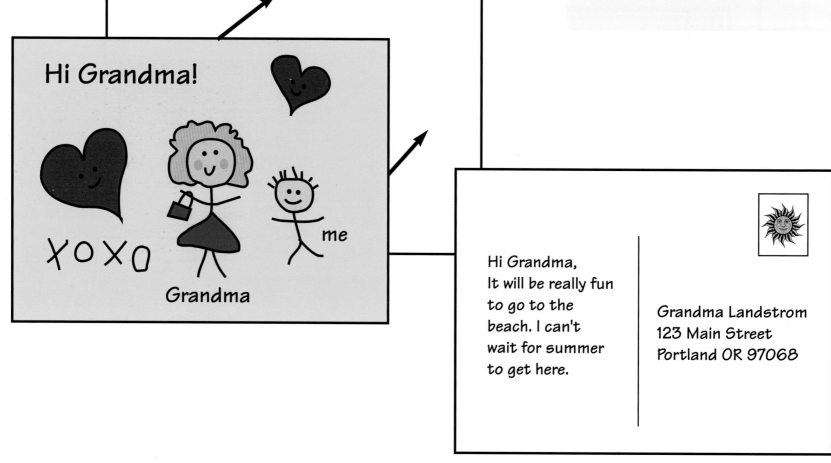

Hi Grandma!

XOXO

Grandma

me

Hi Grandma,
It will be really fun to go to the beach. I can't wait for summer to get here.

Grandma Landstrom
123 Main Street
Portland OR 97068

Crayons and Computers in Cyberspace

Learn more about the ideas in this book by visiting a special Web site. You'll find more art projects and information about color. You can even meet the author of this book and ask her questions. Or, send in your own ideas about using computers for art.

Materials

- **Internet connection**

1. Log on to the Internet and type in this address: http://Members.aol.com/Sabbeth/ CrayonsandComputers.html

Be certain to type this address exactly as it appears with the correct capitalization.

2. Scroll through the page to see the latest project ideas.

3. Send a message to the author by clicking at the bottom of the page.

Create a Cyber Gallery

Your beautiful pictures deserve a gallery all their own.
You can make one on your computer. Have an opening night
party when you display your collection to your friends and family.

There are many ways to make a gallery, depending
on your computer and software.

Pixel Picture Frame

Make this picture frame out of construction paper and tape it around your monitor.

Materials

- **Ruler**
- **Pencil**
- **Construction paper**
- **Scissors**
- **Crayons**
- **Clear plastic tape**

1. Measure the size of your monitor from the very edge of the screen. Note how long it is and how wide the border is all the way around.

2. Cut out 1 construction paper strip to the measurements of each side so that you end up with 4 strips.

3. Use a crayon or marker to draw squiggles on the paper to make it look like a picture frame. Add colors, too.

4. Tape the frame pieces around your computer screen.

Setting up a Picture Gallery

Begin by making a folder on your computer titled "Cyber Gal." Put all your picture files in this folder. The best way to display your work will depend on what type of paint program you have. Here are a few ideas:

If you have Kid Pix Studio: Open the slide show function in Kid Pix Studio and place all your pictures in the show. You can add sound and slide transitions, too. To view your gallery, show the slide show.

If you have ClarisWorks: This program can show each page in a file as one slide in a show. This means that all your artwork has to be in one file, with each picture on a separate page. It's easiest to create your slide show in the Draw program. To set up the slide show in ClarisWorks/Draw, go to the View menu and select "Page View." Go to the Format menu and select "Document." In the area that lists "Pages Down" type in the number of pictures in your show. To place the pictures in the show, open each draw or paint document that has been created. Copy one picture and place it on one page of the slide show. Repeat for all the pieces of art. To see the slide show, go to the View menu and choose "Slide Show." Click on the Start button to begin. Click the mouse to see each slide. To see the slides automatically, choose "Advance every ___ seconds" before you click on Start.

If you don't have a slide show function in your paint program: Try opening all your picture files. Viewers can click on the close box of the top picture when they are ready to see the next one. If you can't open more than one file at a time, open the folder that holds all the files. Each picture can be opened and viewed, one at a time.

Good Old-Fashioned Fun

Have fun learning more about artists, color, and nature the good old-fashioned way. Your library is full of books about famous artists. There are many books written for kids your age. Here are a few you might find interesting and colorful!

Linnea in Monet's Garden by Christina Bjork and Lena Anderson
A Weekend with Picasso by Florian Rodari
A Weekend with van Gogh by Rosabianca Skira-Venturi
Henri Matisse by Mike Venezia

There's nothing like an art museum for seeing the paintings of artists close-up. If you don't have a museum near your home, you might be able to visit one on your next vacation.

A visit to the zoo is a great way to learn more about animals. Many times animals live in settings that look like their real homes. Notice if their colors help them blend into their habitat. Sometimes it's hard to find the lions as they stretch out on their rocky ledges. Maybe you can see a brightly colored poison-dart frog at your zoo. There are also several CD-ROMs about animals.

Zoo Safari Game

Here's a great way to learn about the colors and patterns of animals. Wear these colorful lockets on your next zoo outing. See who can spot his animal pattern first. Being observant is a big part of being an artist. This is a fun game to play while visiting your furry friends.

Materials

- **CD-ROM about zoo animals**
- **Ruler**
- **Computer printer paper**
- **Crayons**
- **Scissors**
- **Pencil**
- **Hole puncher**
- **Yarn**

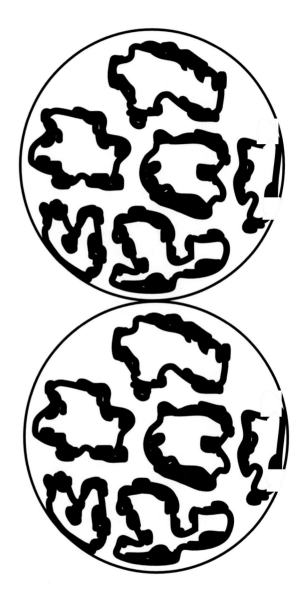

If you don't have a CD-ROM disc drive, take a look at one of the many colorful books about animals. Your library will have a book that has pictures of animals that live in zoos. In it you'll find many patterns and colors to use for this project.

1. Take time to study a CD-ROM or book about zoo animals. Look for animals that have colorful patterns. Some ideas could be a turtle's shell, a leopard's spots, or a coral snake's stripes.

2. At your computer, draw a 3-inch circle. Inside the circle, draw the outline of 1 animal pattern. Copy this and place the new circle above the first, with edges touching. Print 1 copy.

3. Color the pattern so that it matches the animal it belongs to. Cut both circles out in 1 piece. Fold the piece in half, bending it on the area where the circles touch, so that the artwork faces out. Write the name of the animal in pencil on the inside of this locket.

4. Punch a hole near the locket's fold. Thread a 40-inch piece of yarn through the hole. Tie the ends of the yarn together.

Repeat these steps to make a different animal pattern locket for everyone in your family.

5. To play the game, give everyone a locket to wear at the zoo. Go on a safari to find the patterns you have drawn. If someone thinks she has spotted her animal, open the locket to see if she is correct.

Leopard

Bibliography

Cole, Alison. *Color*. London: Dorling Kindersley, 1993.

Fanning, Jim. *Walt Disney*. New York: Chelsea House Publishers, 1994.

Ferrier, Jean-Louis. *The Fauves*. Paris: Terrail, 1995.

Hellman, Hal. *The Art and Science of Color*. New York: McGraw—Hill Book Company, 1967.

Leland, Nita. *Exploring Color*. Cincinnati: North Light Publishers, 1985.

Parramon, Jose. *The Book of Color*. New York: Watson-Guptill Publications, 1993.

Thomson, Belinda, and Michael Howard. *Impressionism*. New York: Smithmark Publishers, 1992.

Index

Kids' Activity Books the Whole Family Can Enjoy

Big Book of Fun
Creative Learning Activities for Home & School, Ages 4–12
Carolyn Buhai Haas
Illustrated by Jane Bennet Phillips
Includes more than 200 projects and activities—from indoor-outdoor games and nature crafts to holiday ideas, cooking fun, and much more.
ISBN 1-55652-020-4
280 pages, paper, $14.95

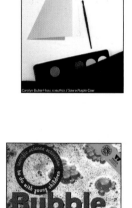

Days of Knights and Damsels
An Activity Guide
Laurie Carlson
Kids can re-create a long-ago world of kings, castles, jousts, jesters, magic fairies, and Robin Hood—all they need are their imaginations and materials they can find at home.
ages 5–12
ISBN 1-55652-291-6
184 pages, paper, $14.95

Bubble Monster
And Other Science Fun
John Falk, Robert L. Pruitt II, Kristi S. Rosenberg, and Tali A. Katz
Forty-five fun science activities created by the ScienceMinders project of the YWCA of Annapolis and Anne Arundel County.
ages 3–8
ISBN 1-55652-301-7
176 pages, paper, $17.95

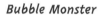

Frank Lloyd Wright for Kids
Kathleen Thorne-Thomsen
A thorough biography is followed by stimulating projects that enable kids to grasp the ideas underlying Wright's work—and have fun in the process.
ages 8 & up
ISBN 1-55652-207-X
144 pages, paper, $14.95

Colonial Kids
An Activity Guide to Life in the New World
Laurie Carlson
Young adventurers can learn about the settling of America while enjoying activities like stitching a sampler, pitching horseshoes, making an almanac, churning butter, and more.
ages 5–12
ISBN 1-55652-322-X
152 pages, paper, $12.95

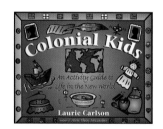

Green Thumbs
A Kid's Activity Guide to Indoor and Outdoor Gardening
Laurie Carlson
With a few seeds, some water and soil, and this book, kids will be creating gardens of their own in no time. They will also create compost, make watering cans, mix-up bug sprays, lay slug traps, grow crazy cucumbers, and much more.
ages 5–12
ISBN 1-55652-238-X
144 pages, paper, $12.95

Kids Camp!
Activities for the Backyard or Wilderness
Laurie Carlson and Judith Dammel
Young campers will build an awareness of the environment, learn about insect and animal behavior, boost their self-esteem, and acquire all the basic skills for fun, successful camping.
ages 5–12
ISBN 1-55652-237-1
184 pages, paper, $12.95

Kids Celebrate!
Activities for Special Days Throughout the Year
Maria Bonfanti Esche and Clare Bonfanti Braham
Illustrations by Mary Jones
The significance of 100 different celebratory days is thoroughly explained as 200 related activities pay charming, educational tribute to the holidays, history, and accomplishments of many cultures and many people.
ages 3–9
ISBN 1-55652-292-4
228 pages, paper, $16.95

Loaves of Fun
A History of Bread with Activities and Recipes from Around the World
Elizabeth M. Harbison
Illustrated by John Harbison
More than thirty recipes and activities take kids on a multicultural journey to discover bread and the people who created, cooked, ate, and enjoyed it.
ages 6–12
ISBN 1-55652-311-4
110 pages, paper, $12.95

Look at Me
Creative Learning Activities for Babies and Toddlers
Carolyn Buhai Haas
Illustrated by Jane Bennett Phillips
Activities for babies and toddlers that inspire creativity and learning through play.
ISBN 1-55652-021-2
228 pages, paper, $11.95

More Than Moccasins
A Kid's Activity Guide to Traditional North American Indian Life
Laurie Carlson
Kids will discover traditions and skills handed down from the people who first settled this continent, including how to plant a garden, make useful pottery, and communicate through Navajo code talkers.
ages 5–12
ISBN 1-55652-213-4
200 pages, paper, $12.95

My Own Fun
Creative Learning Activities for Home and School
Carolyn Buhai Haas and Anita Cross Friedman
More than 160 creative learning projects and activities for elementary-school children.
ages 7–12
ISBN 1-55652-093-X
194 pages, paper, $9.95

On Stage
Theater Games and Activities for Kids
Lisa Bany-Winters
Have fun over the footlights while playing theater games, learning about puppetry and pantomime, making sound effects, costumes, props, and scenery, applying stage makeup; and more. Several play scripts are included.
ages 6–12
ISBN 1-55652-324-6
160 pages, paper, $14.95

Sandbox Scientist
Real Science Activities for Little Kids
Michael E. Ross
Illustrated by Mary Anne Lloyd
Parents, teachers, and day-care leaders learn to assemble "Explorer Kits" that will send kids off on their own investigations, in groups or individually, with a minimum of adult intervention.
ages 2–8
ISBN 1-55652-248-7
208 pages, paper, $12.95

Shaker Children
True Stories and Crafts
Kathleen Thorne-Thomsen
This charming book combines two true biographies and authentic activities to tell children of today about the Shakers of yesterday.
ages 8 & up
ISBN 1-55652-250-9
128 pages, paper, $15.95

Splish Splash
Water Fun for Kids
Penny Warner
Kids love water—whether it's the ocean, lake, pool, or backyard sprinkler. Here are more than 120 ideas for water fun for toddlers to teens.
ages 2—12
ISBN 1-55652-262-2
176 pages, paper, $12.95

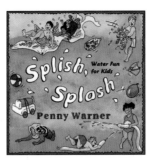

Why Design?
Projects from the National Building Museum
Anna Slafer and Kevin Cahill
Containing photographs, illustrations, work sheets, and lists of questions for more than forty projects, this book will stimulate anyone interested in design.
ages 12 & up
ISBN 1-55652-249-5
208 pages, paper, $19.95

Westward Ho!
An Activity Guide to the Wild West
Laurie Carlson
Cowboys and cowgirls explore the West with activities such as sewing a sunbonnet, panning for gold, cooking flapjacks, singing cowboy songs, and much more.
ages 5—12
ISBN 1-55652-271-1
160 pages, paper, $12.95

The Wind at Work
An Activity Guide to Windmills
Gretchen Woelfle
With more than a dozen wind-related activities and more than 100 photos, line drawings, charts, and graphs, this book traces the history of windmills and how their design and function have changed over time.
ages 8—13
ISBN 1-55652-308-4
144 pages, paper, $14.95

About the Author

Carol Sabbeth has been exploring creative ways to use computers for years. In her workshops, kids use their creativity while making computer arts and crafts projects. Masterpieces start out on the computer and end up as finished works of art made of paper, soap, fabric, and paint. Carol lives in Carmel, California where she teaches children and teachers to use the computer as an artist's tool.

Carol lives with three very colorful characters, Dieter Bird, Big Cat, and Alex, her husband.